Wind River Range

impressions

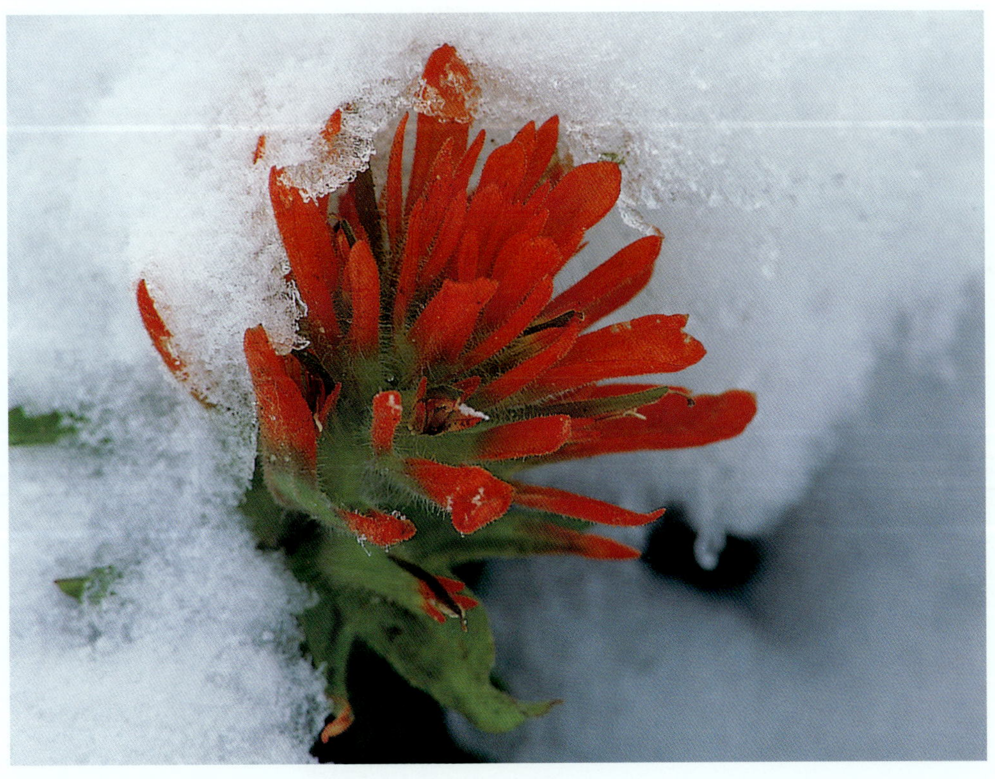

photography by Fred Pflughoft and others

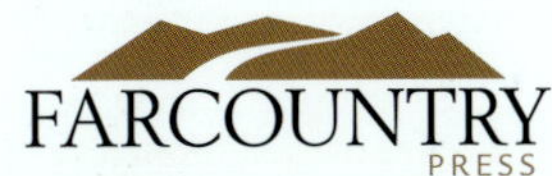

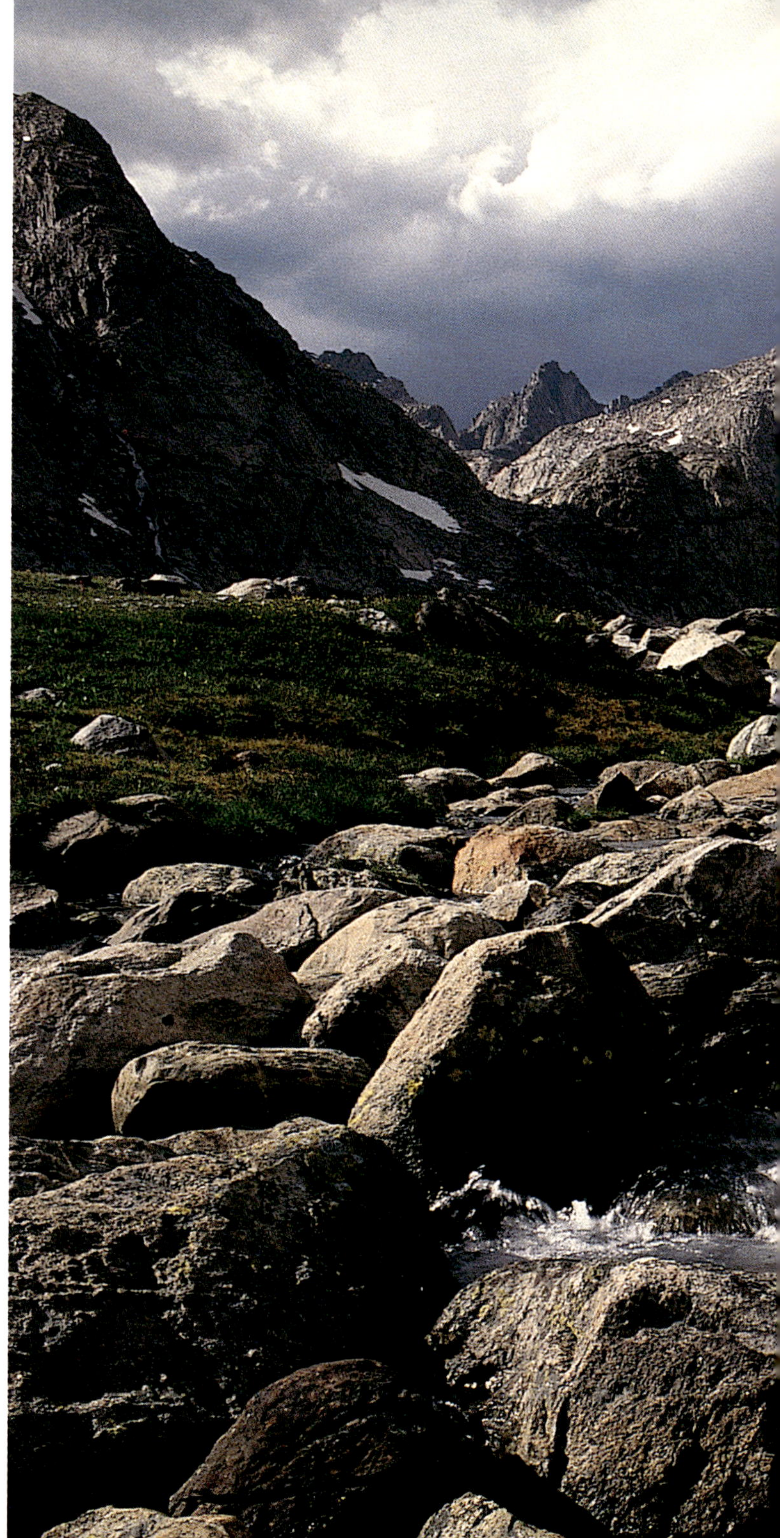

Right: Stream tumbles out of Titcomb Basin.
FRED PFLUGHOFT

Title page: Paintbrush and June snow.
ELIZABETH BOEHM

Front cover: Squaretop Mountain above Green River Lakes.
FRED PFLUGHOFT

Back cover: Shoreline of Upper Green River Lake.
ELIZABETH BOEHM

ISBN 1-56037-291-5

Created, produced, and designed in the United States.
Printed in China.

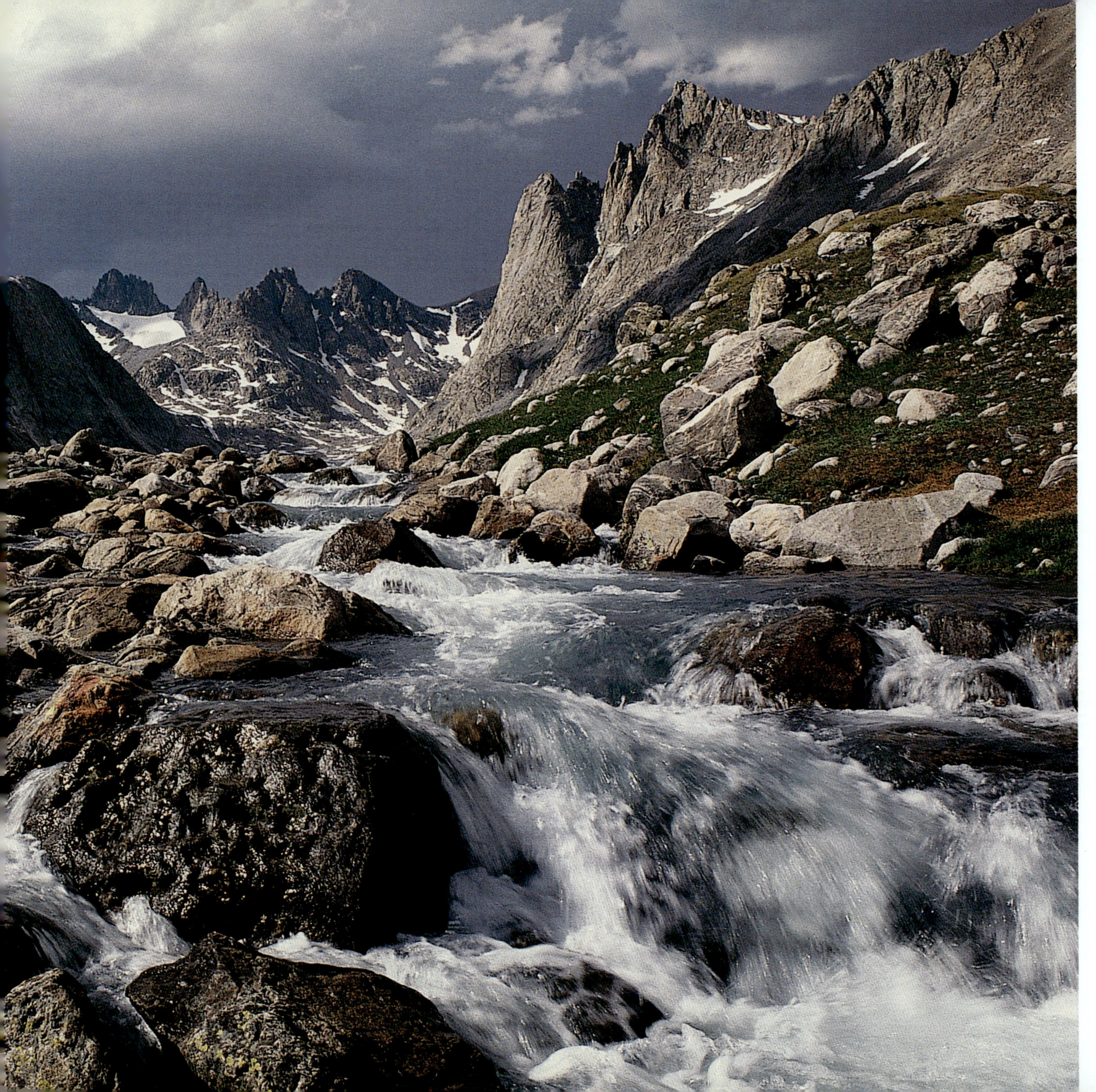

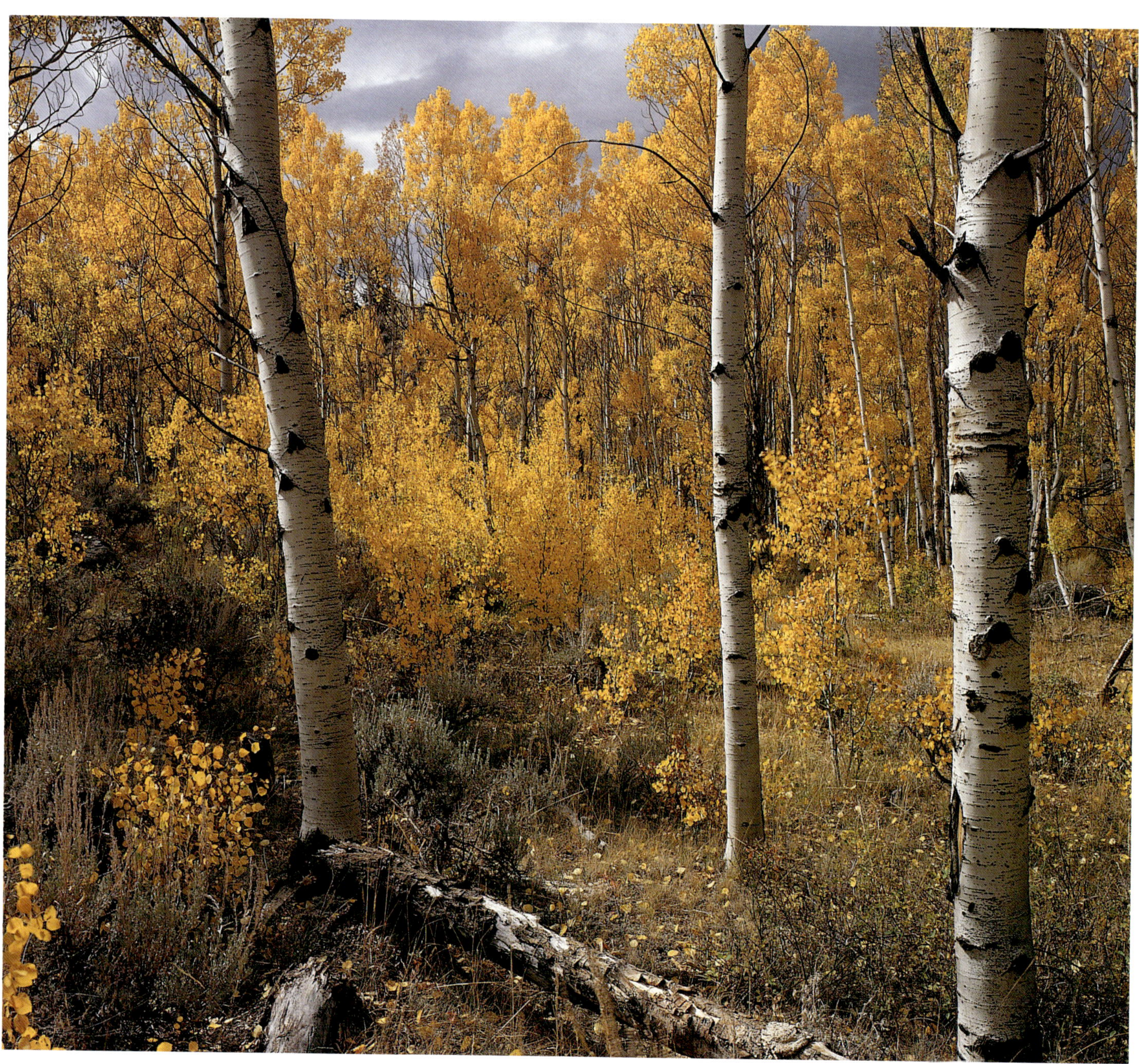

INTRODUCTION

by Fred Pflughoft

When I was asked to write this introduction, the first thought that came into my mind was, what superlatives could I use to do this special place justice. In my lifetime of travel and countless miles of hiking, backpacking, and climbing, I have found no other place quite like the Wind River Range—a place of grandeur, awe-inspiring beauty, and perpetual mystery.

The grandeur of the Wind River Range begins in the northwestern part of Wyoming near Togwotee Pass and extends roughly 110 miles—as the crow flies—in a southeasterly direction. The range encompasses the jagged crest of the Continental Divide and averages about 25 miles in width as it heads toward South Pass and its terminus. Along the way these mountains pass through one of the largest roadless tracts of land in the lower forty-eight states. Four huge wilderness areas have been set aside to protect the more pristine part of this range and they effectively limit access by all but the hardy and adventurous souls who come here seeking an escape from the frantic pace of life. As you enter this vast domain of precipitous towers, tranquil waters, and unending vistas you can't help but leave behind the cares of life on the outside, only to be absorbed by the rhythm of life on the inside—inside one of the grandest places on earth.

Everywhere you gaze there is a feast of awe-inspiring beauty. From the immense glacier-carved lakes framed by rock-strewn morainal ridges to the towering castles of fault-block stone covered with snow and ice, there is a special beauty for every eye to behold. For those who explore this region, that beauty can also be found while walking along one of the countless streams that cascade tumultuously out of this rugged country, hiking a Technicolor, flower-carpeted meadow high above treeline, watching a spectacular sunset from the shore of an alpine lake, or standing on the apex of a cathedral of rock with miles of stunning vistas spread out below.

After twenty years I am still unable to explain wholly why the Wind River Range—the Winds—has such an allure for me and countless others I know. After all, there are other great mountain ranges in the United States: the North Cascades, the Sierras, and the San Juans, to name but a few. But mention the Winds to an avid backpacker or climber and invariably you will catch a special glint in his or her eye or a change in demeanor as to indicate there is something different about this place. I first journeyed to this region of high peaks with my wife Sue on our first major backpacking trip together in 1981. After ten adventure-filled days we were hooked. For the next ten years we spent our summer vacation hiking and climbing in the high reaches of the northern portion of the range. Finally, after fifteen years, we just packed up and moved our family to the foot of the mountains that had so mesmerized us. It is still a mystery to me why we did. But as I take my daily walk on top of one of the terminal moraines that holds back the waters of beautiful Fremont Lake and I gaze at the jagged skyline of peaks that so long ago captured my imagination, I can't help but sense there is a very good explanation. And if it remains a mystery, that's alright; it will give me reason to continue to seek out answers along the streams, in the forests and meadows, and on the summits that make up this very special place.

I hope you enjoy what I have found so far and realize that my images take in only what I have personally experienced to date. Because of the vastness of the Winds, I found it necessary to gather images from others who feel as I do about this beautiful area. I believe the essence of this book can be found in the variety of photographic styles and subjects represented here; in a very real sense this collection portrays the diversity of this grand ecosystem, showing both the beauty and mystery of the Wind River Range.

Facing page: Fall aspens across from Half Moon Lake Overlook, Bridger-Teton National Forest. FRED PFLUGHOFT

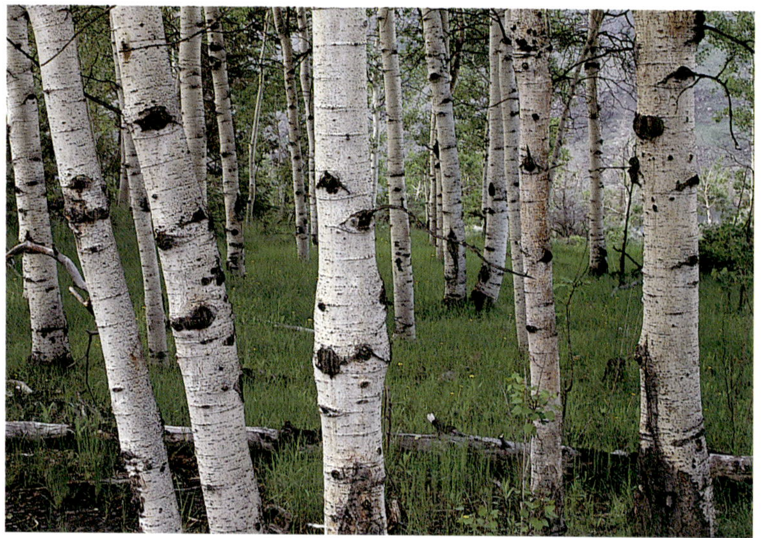

Above: Aspens near Boulder Lake, Bridger-Teton National Forest. *FRED PFLUGHOFT*

Right: Pipestone Creek tumbles through the Wind River Mountains, Bridger Wilderness. *DELSA SMITH ALLEN*

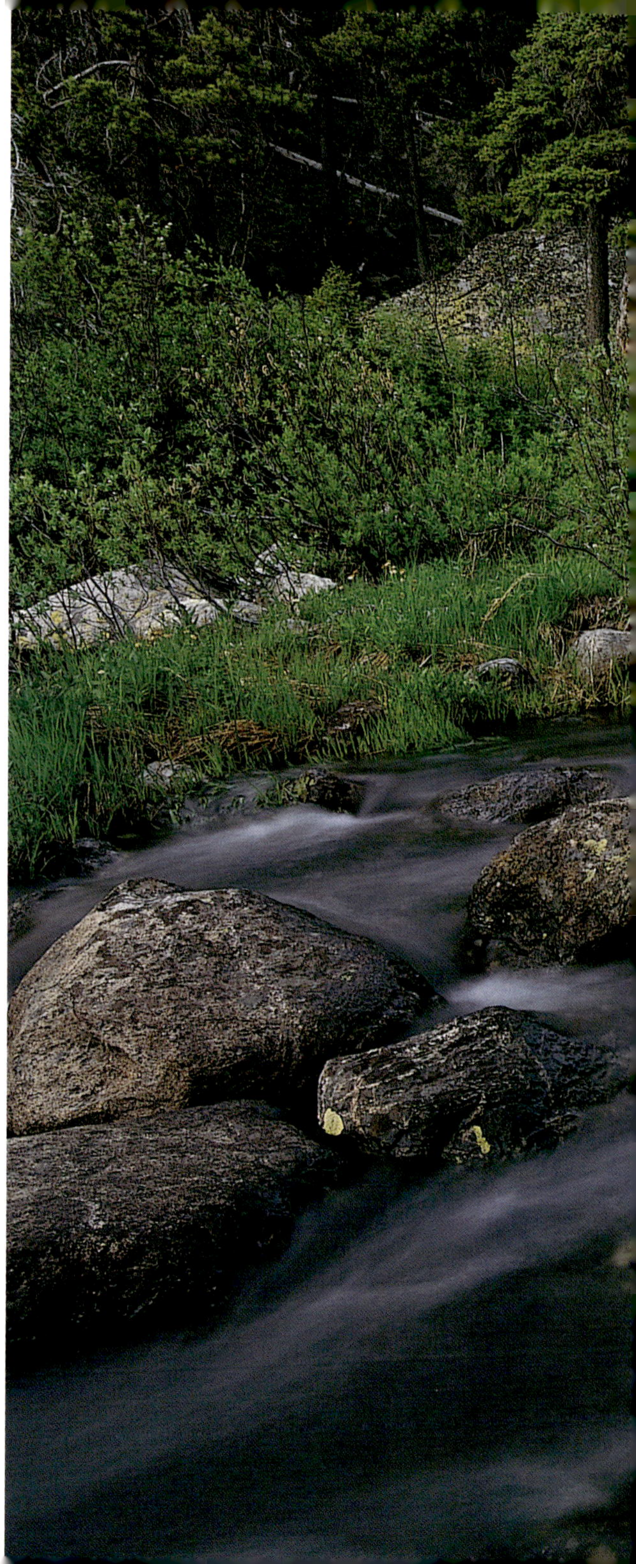

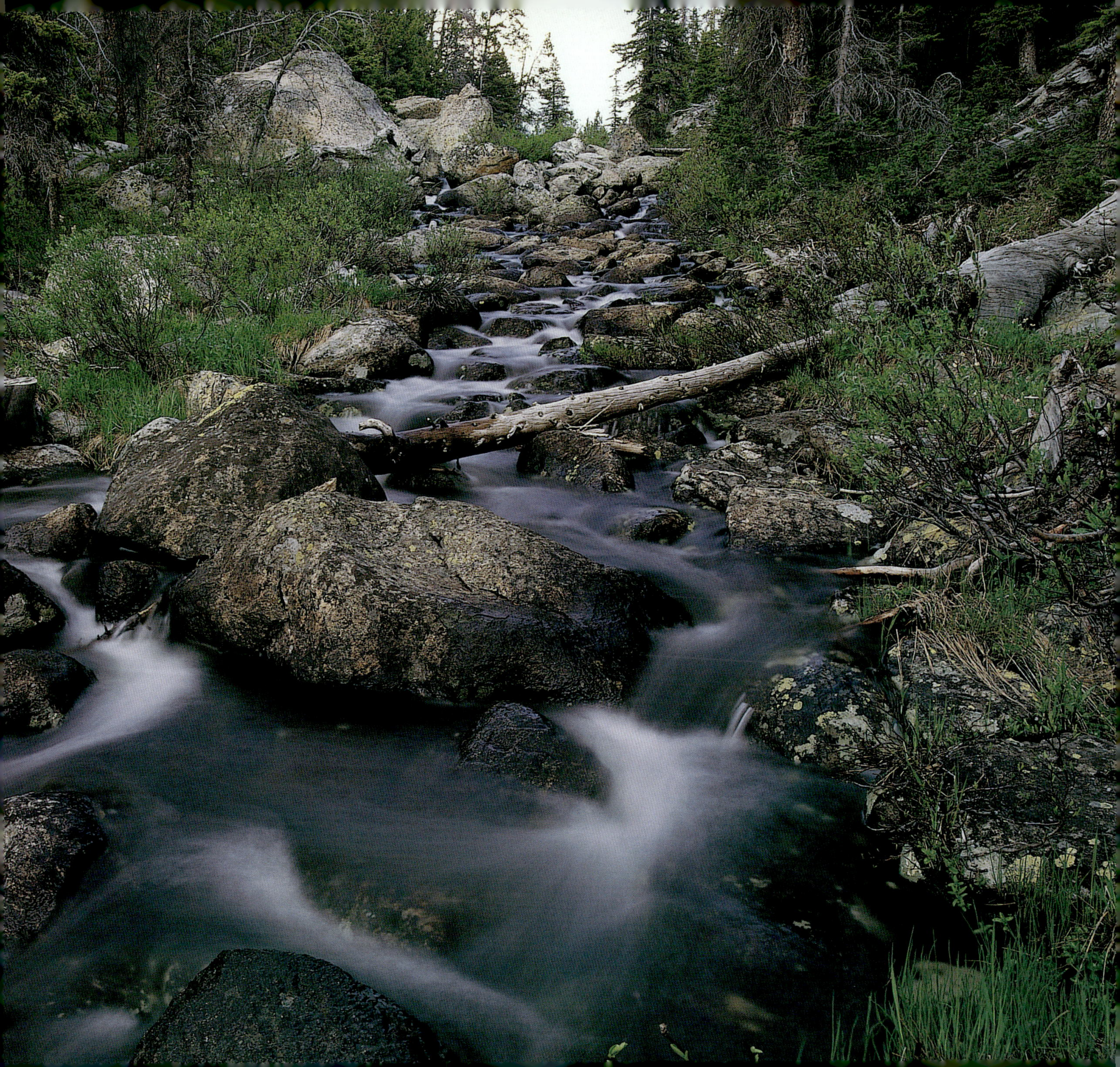

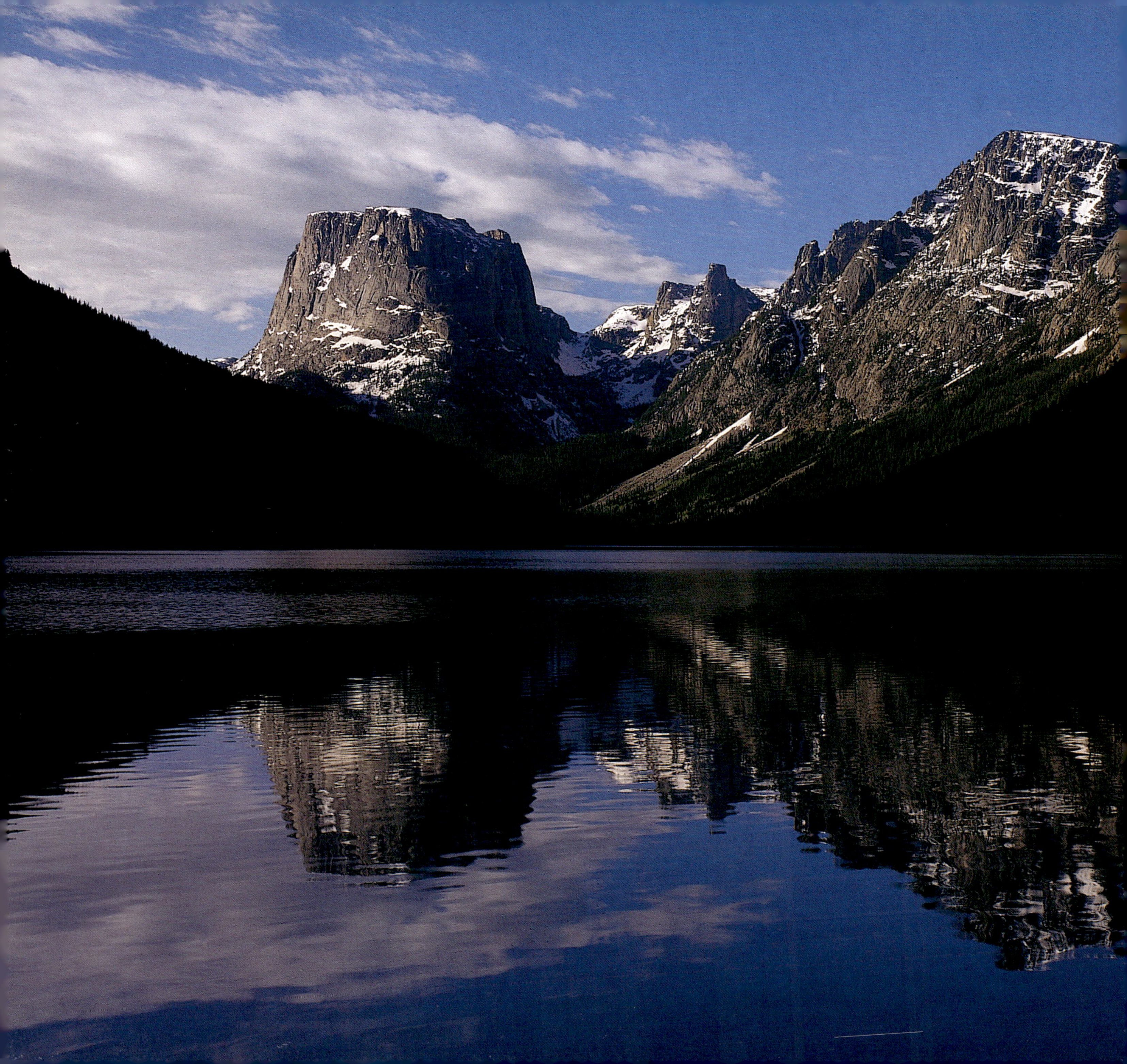

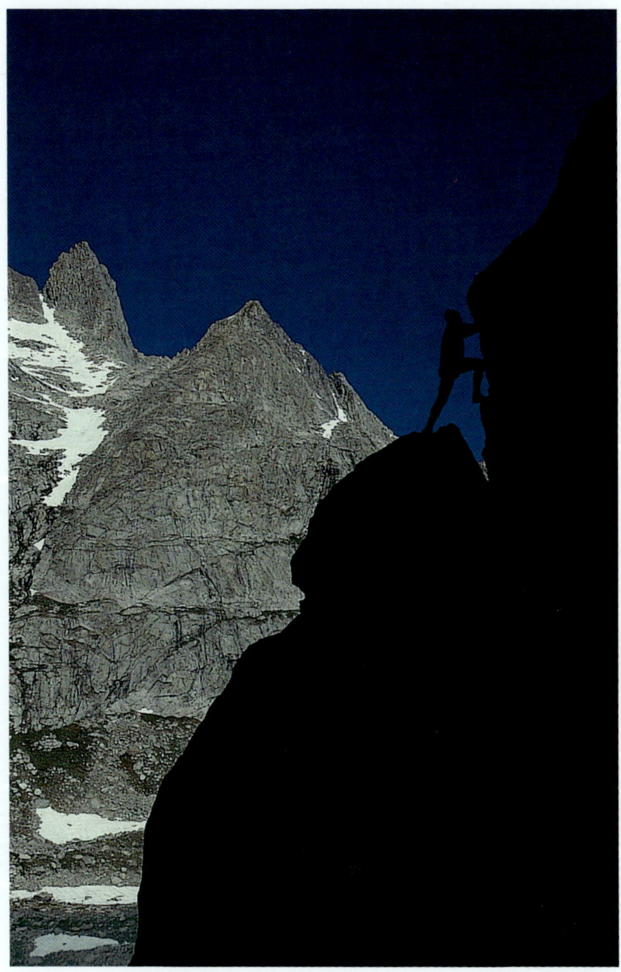

Above: Bouldering in Titcomb Basin.
FRED PFLUGHOFT

Left: Squaretop Mountain reflected in Upper Green River Lake.
FRED PFLUGHOFT

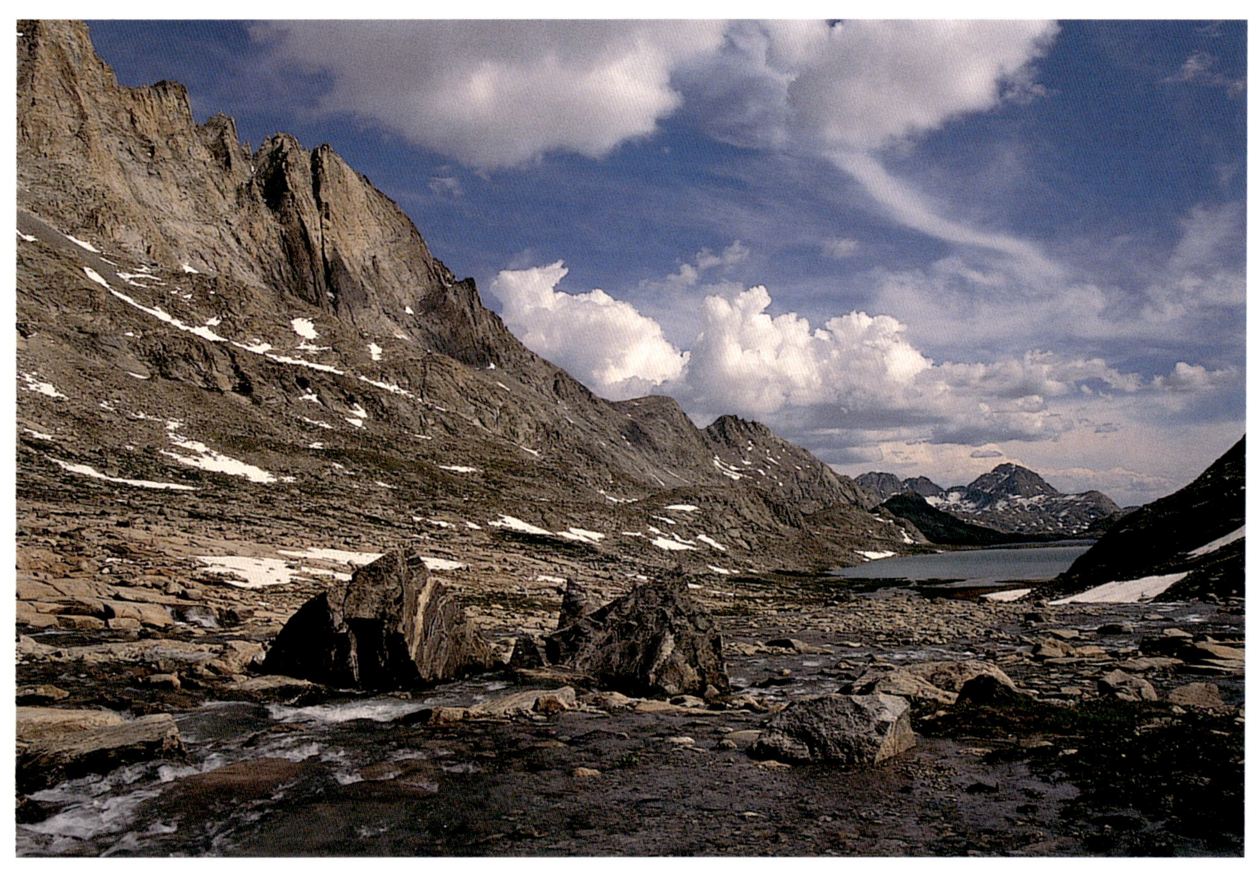

Above: View of 13,745-foot Fremont Peak and Upper Titcomb Lake from Titcomb Basin.
FRED PFLUGHOFT

Facing page: Cirque of the Towers rises above Jackass Pass.
FRED PFLUGHOFT

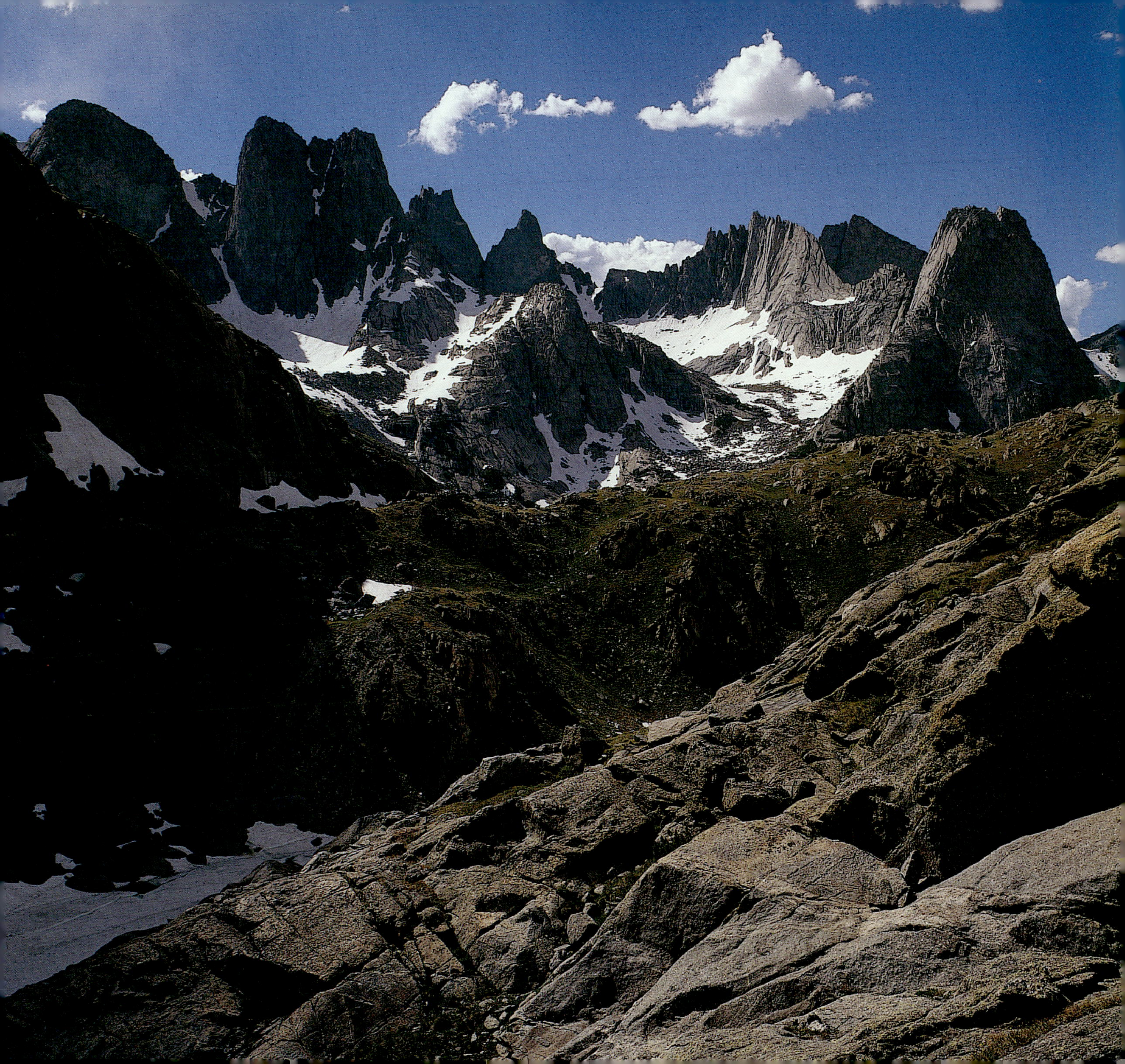

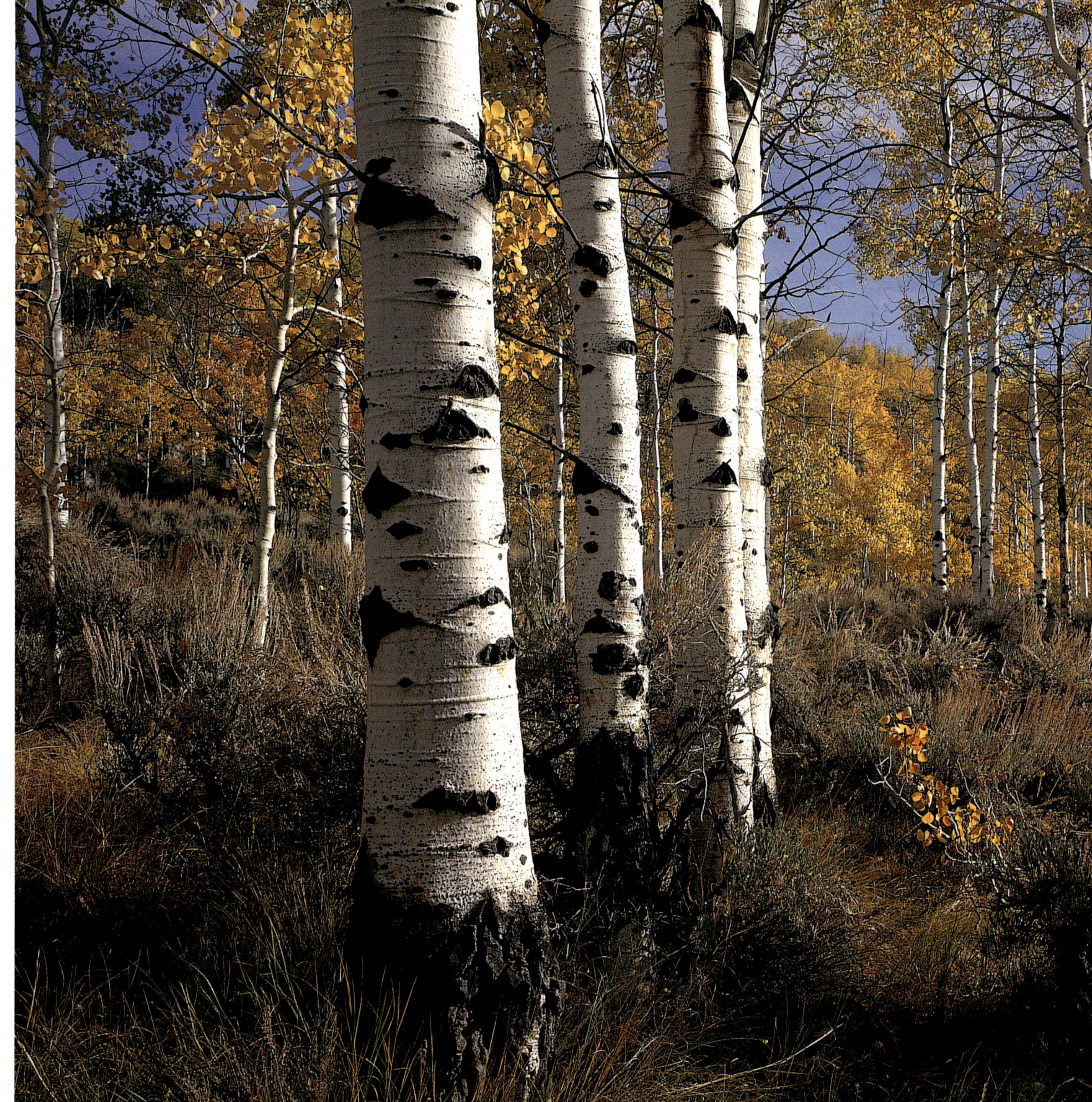

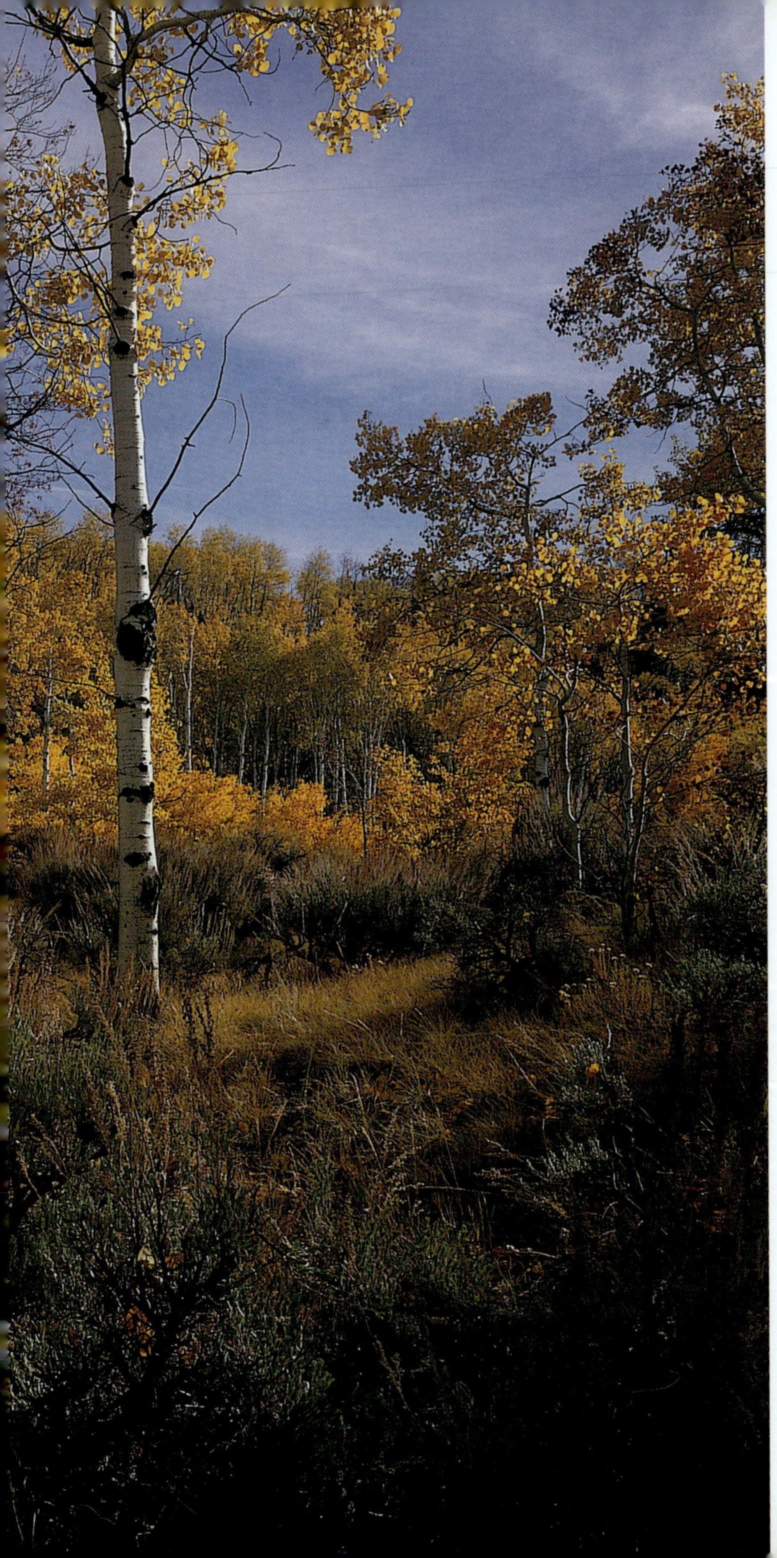

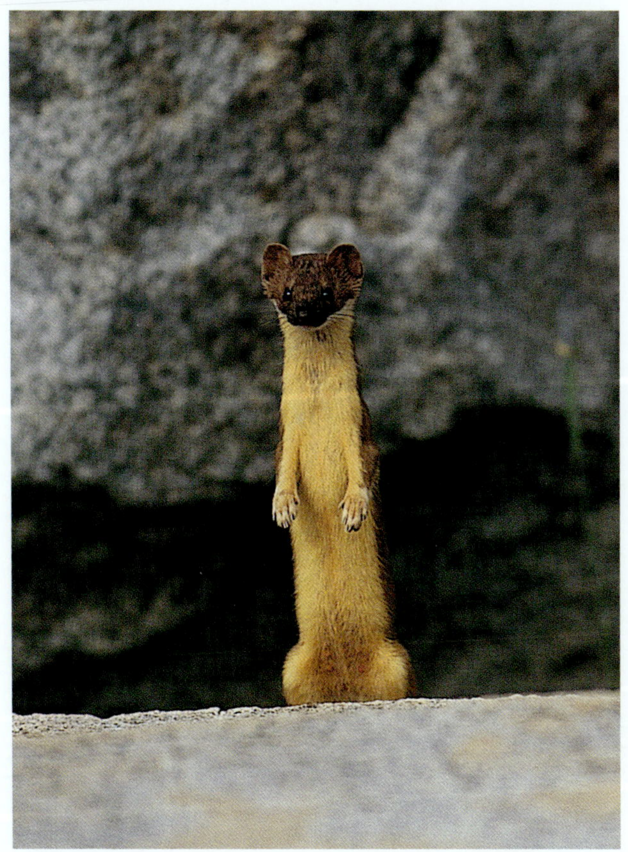

Above: Weasel on alert.
ELIZABETH BOEHM

Left: An aspen grove near Half Moon Lake Campground ablaze in fall color, Bridger-Teton National Forest.
FRED PFLUGHOFT

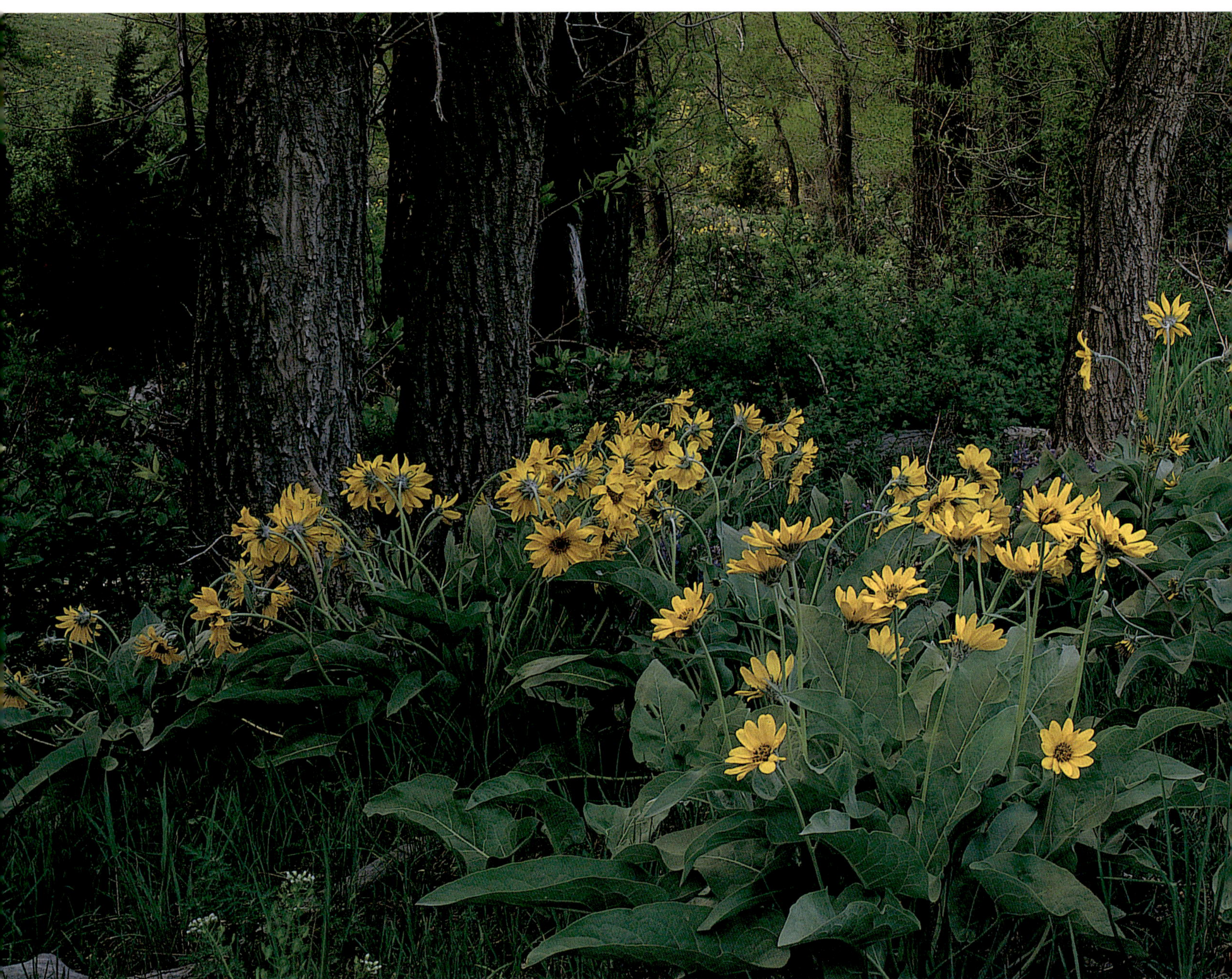

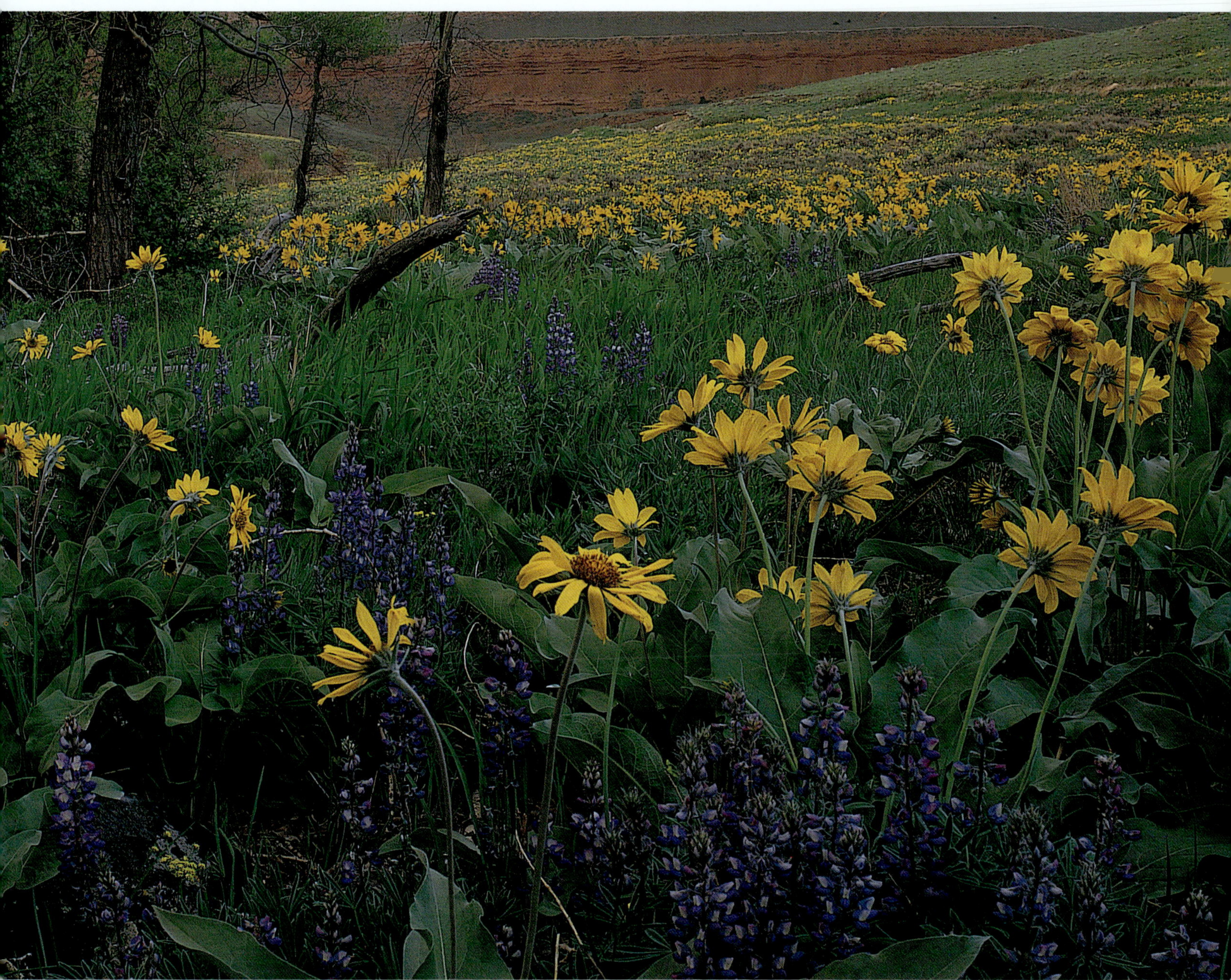

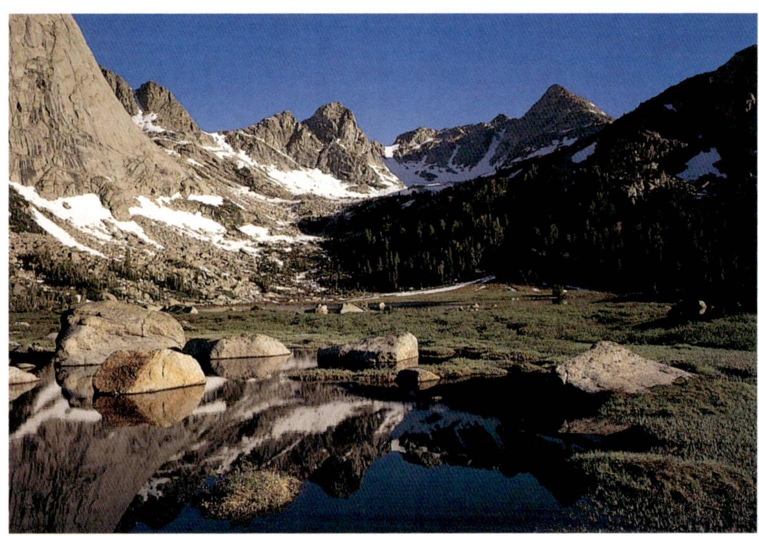

Above: Texas Pass and Camels Hump above Lonesome Lake, Popo Agie Wilderness. *FRED PFLUGHOFT*

Right: Sky Pilot reflected in small tarn near Elbow Lake. *FRED PFLUGHOFT*

Preceding pages: Lupine mingles with arrow-leaved balsamroot in Red Canyon near Lander. *FRED PFLUGHOFT*

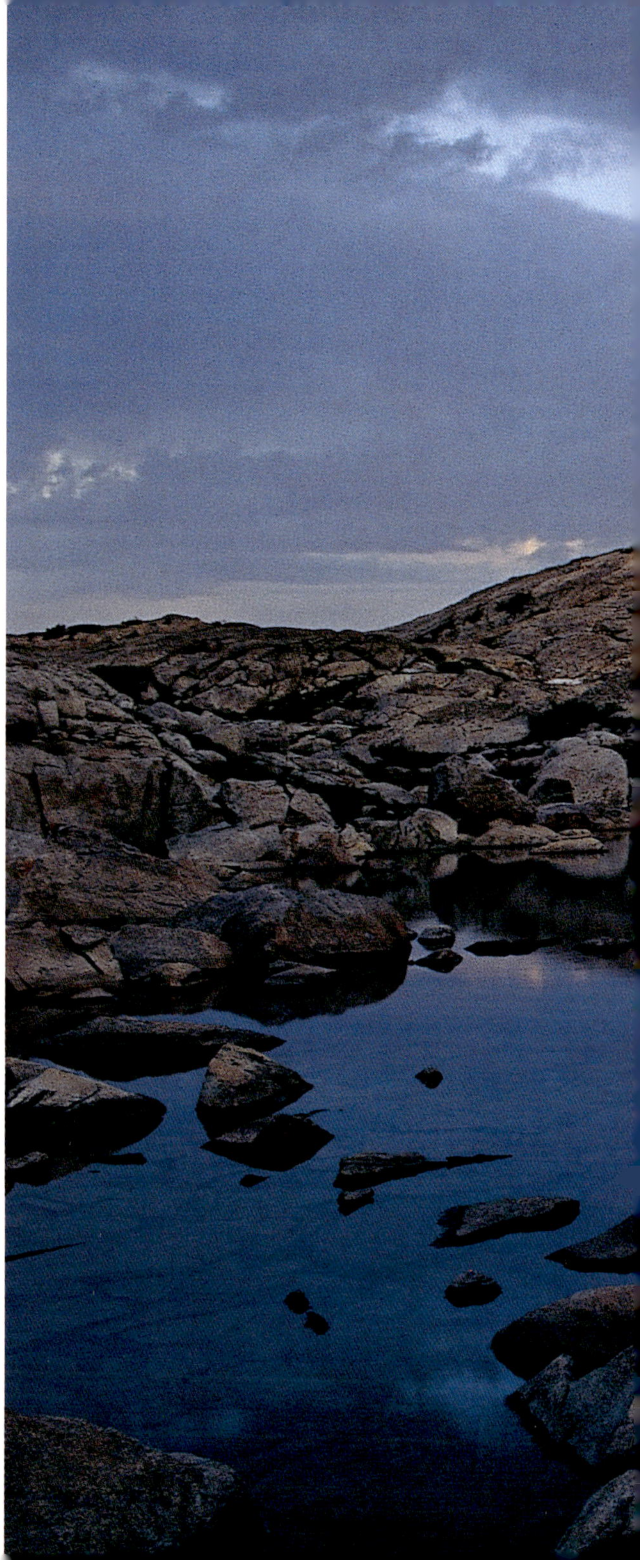

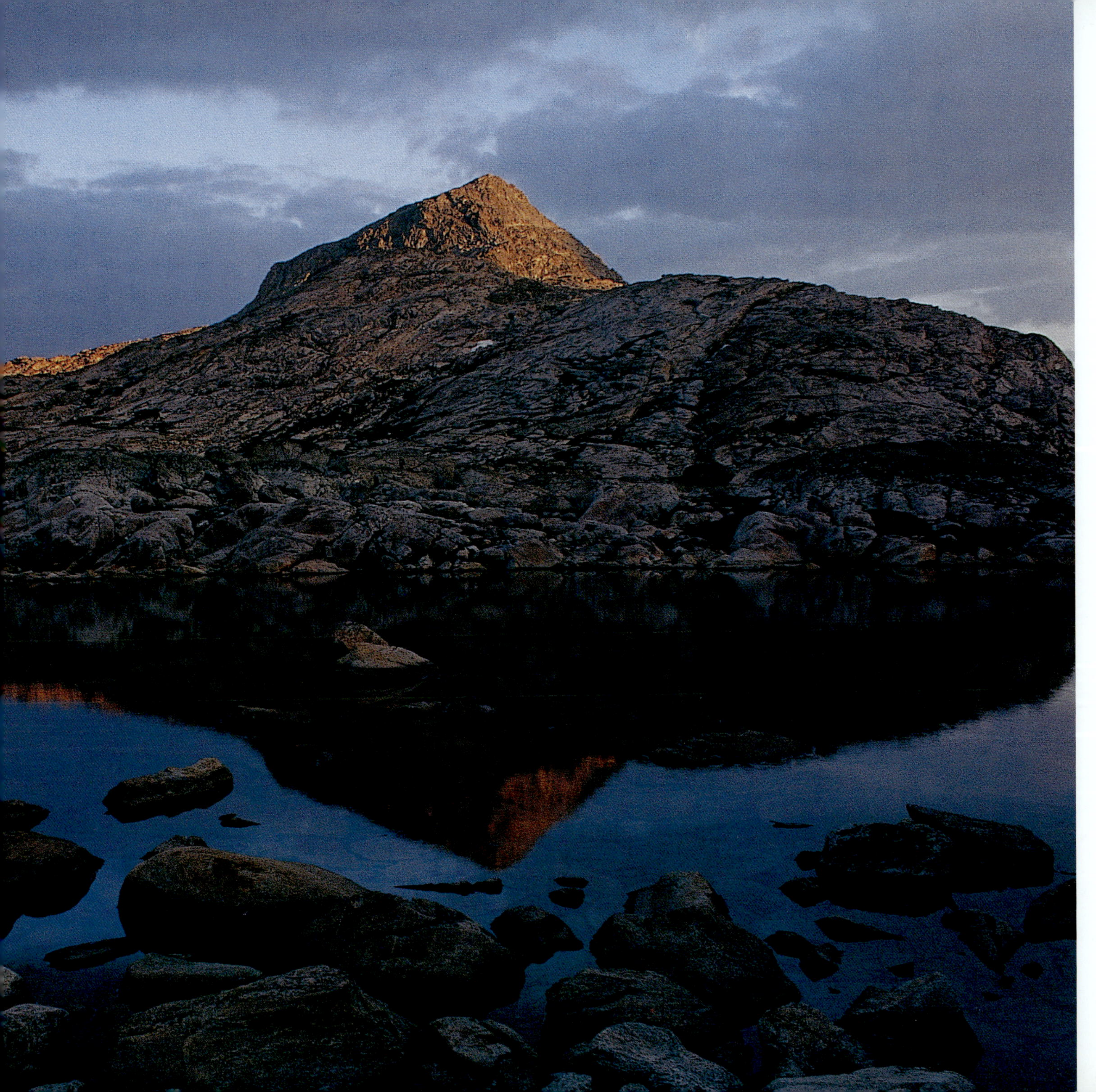

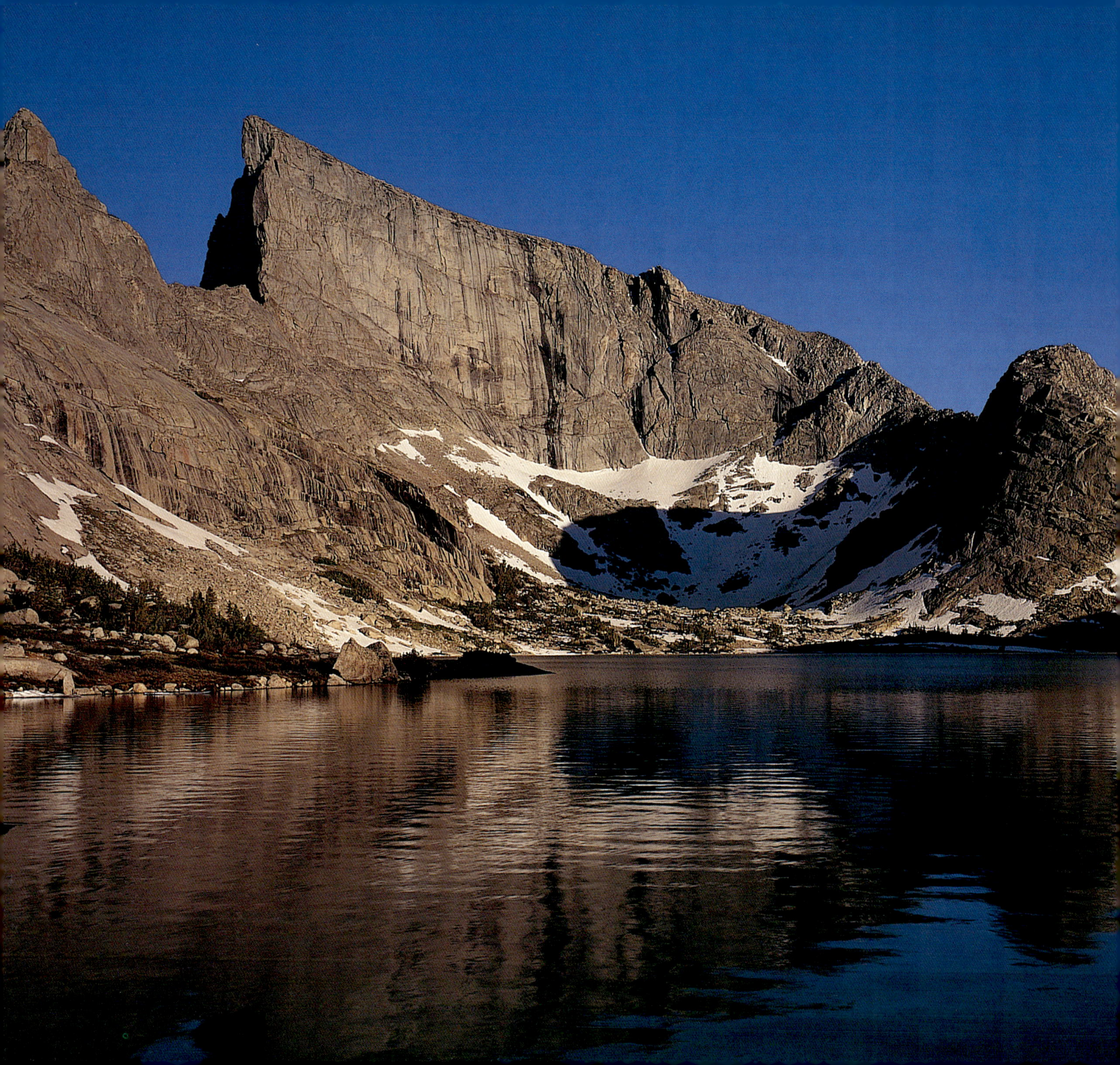

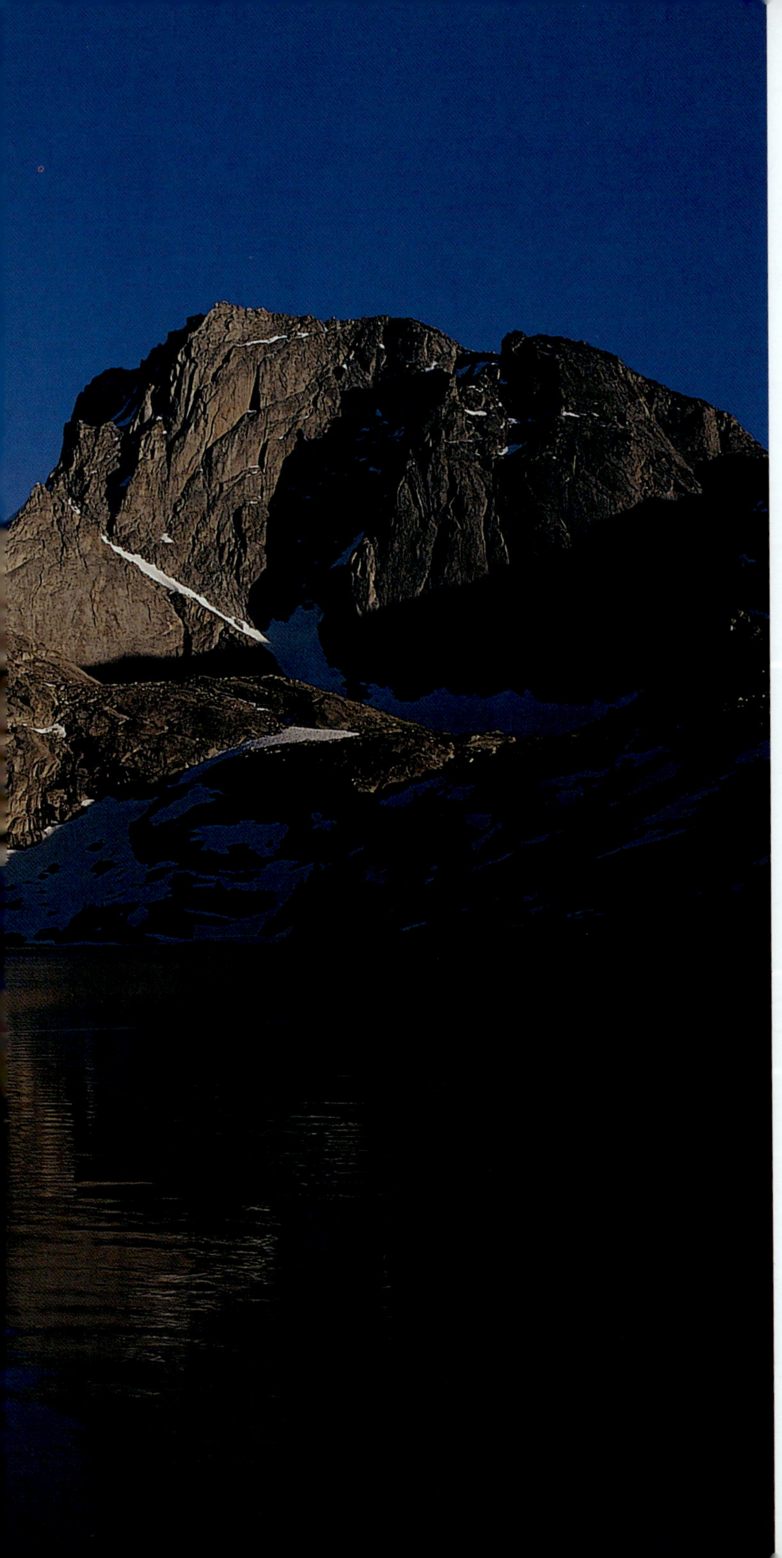

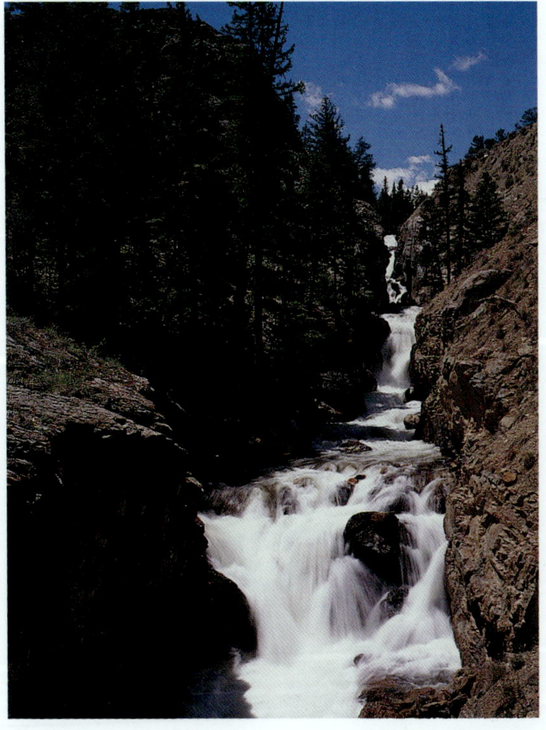

Above: Torrey Creek tumbles out of the Wind River Mountains. *FRED PFLUGHOFT*

Left: East Temple and Temple peaks seem to gaze at their own reflections in Deep Lake. *FRED PFLUGHOFT*

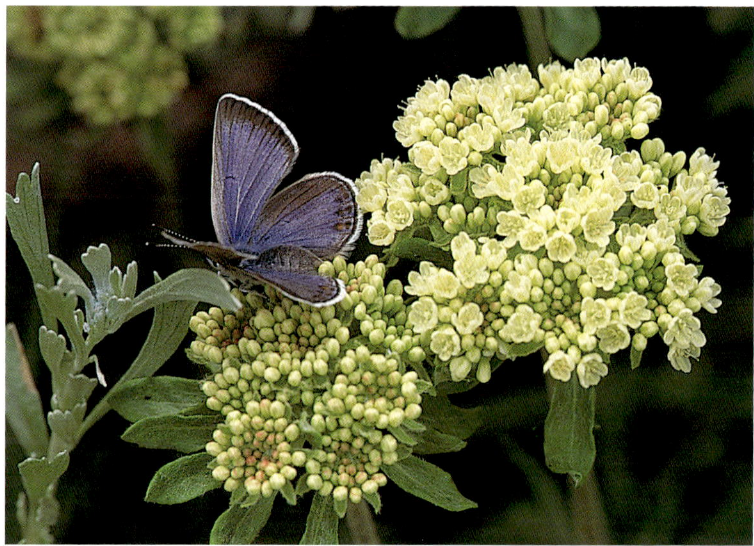

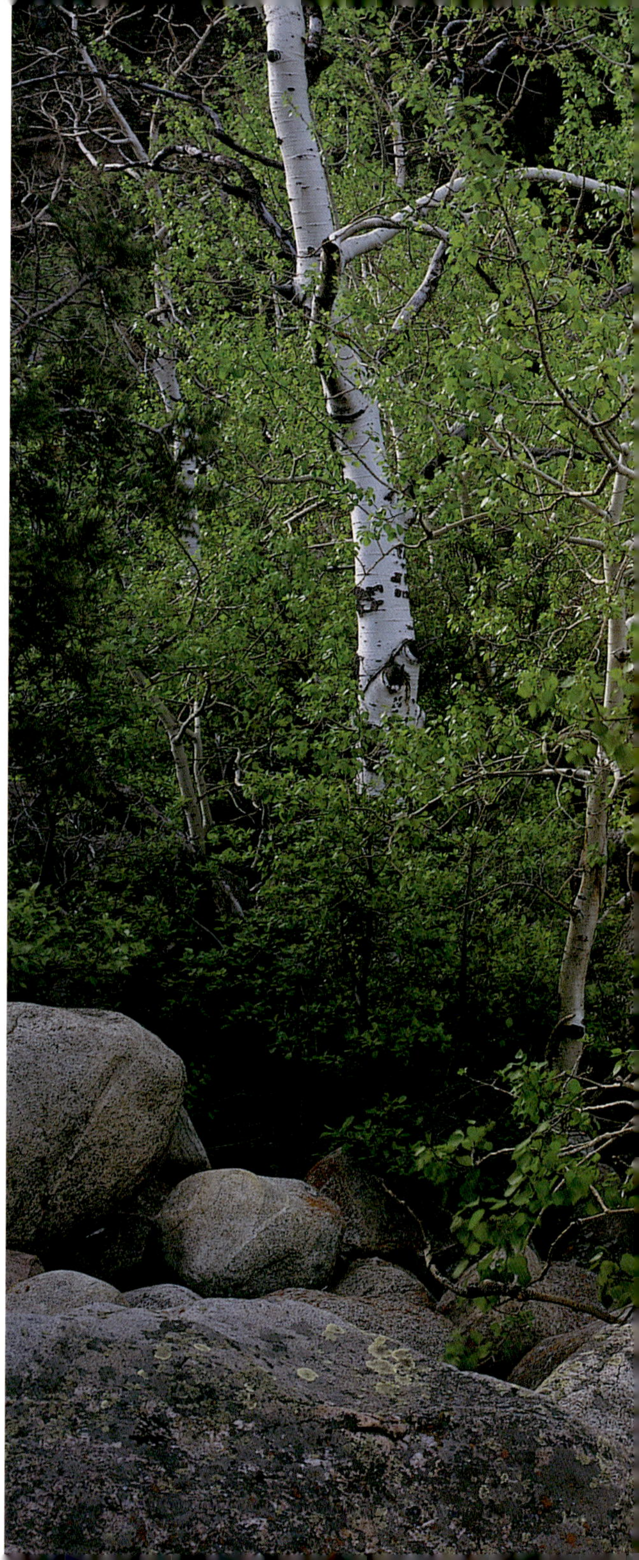

Above: Blue copper butterfly alights on its favorite food, buckwheat. *ELIZABETH BOEHM*

Right: "The sinks," the portion of the Popo Agie River that "sinks" into limestone fissures. The river then re-emerges at "the rise" warmer and in greater volume, suggesting the presence of underground springs in the limestone cavern, Sinks Canyon State Park. *FRED PFLUGHOFT*

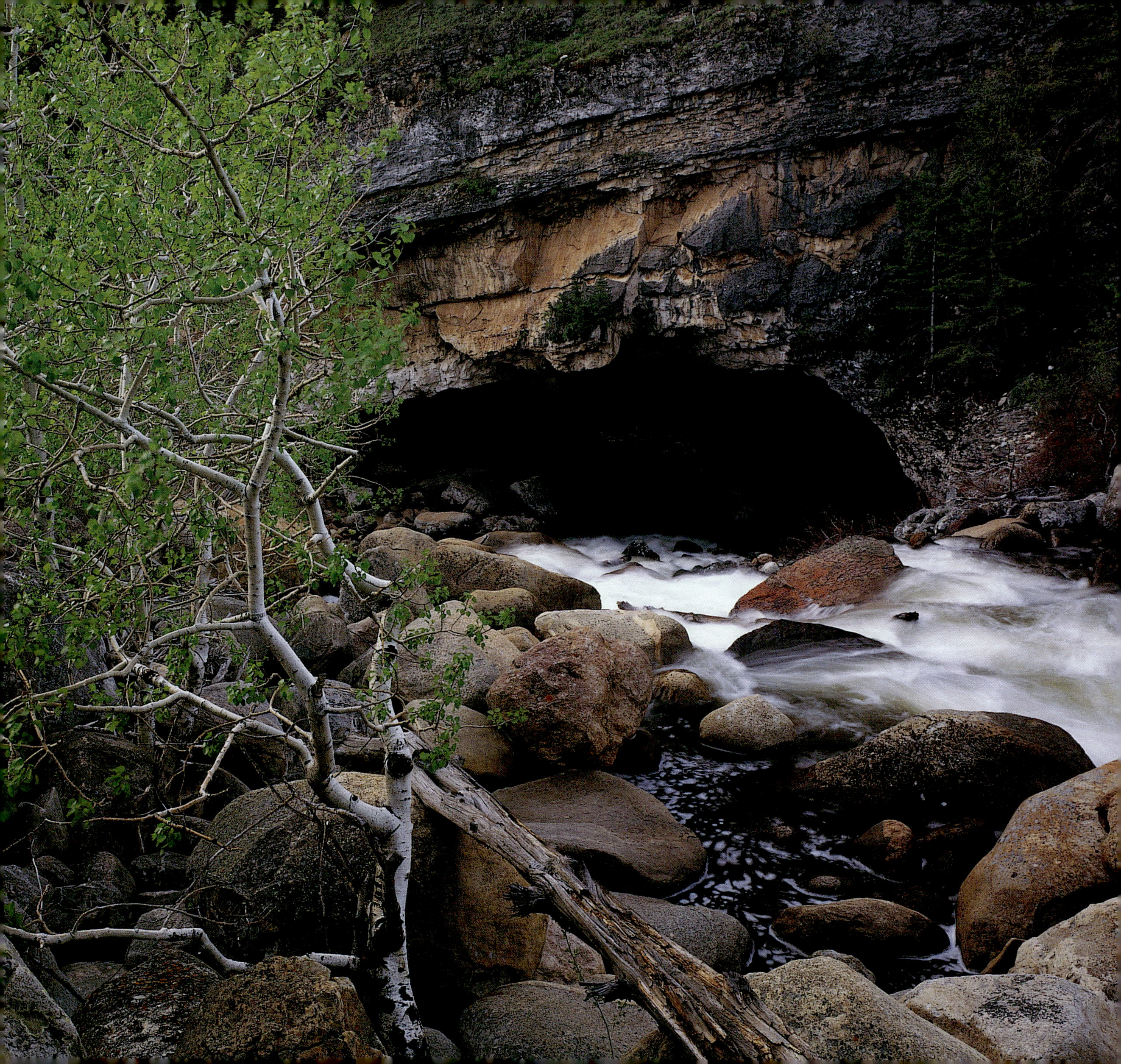

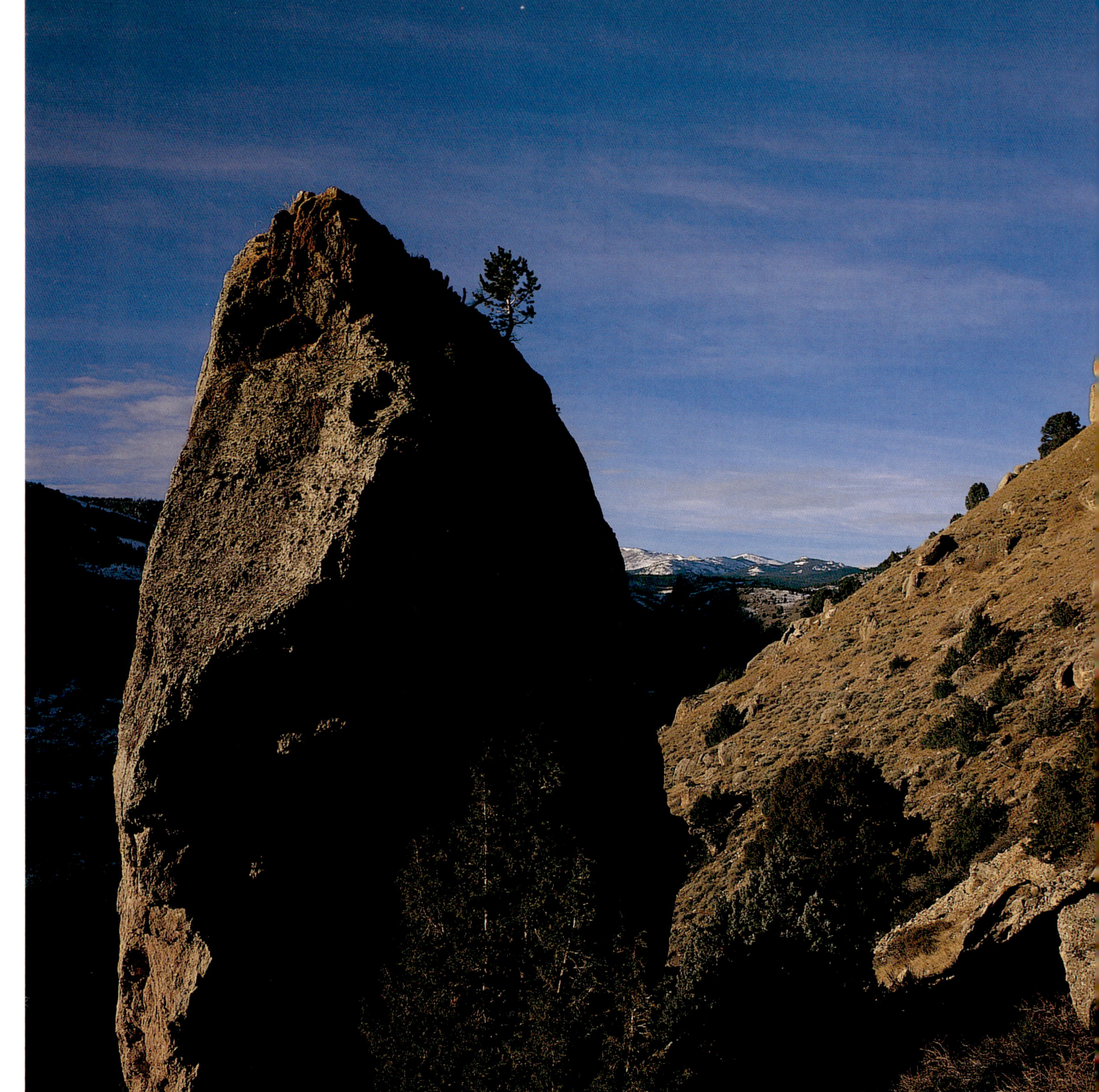

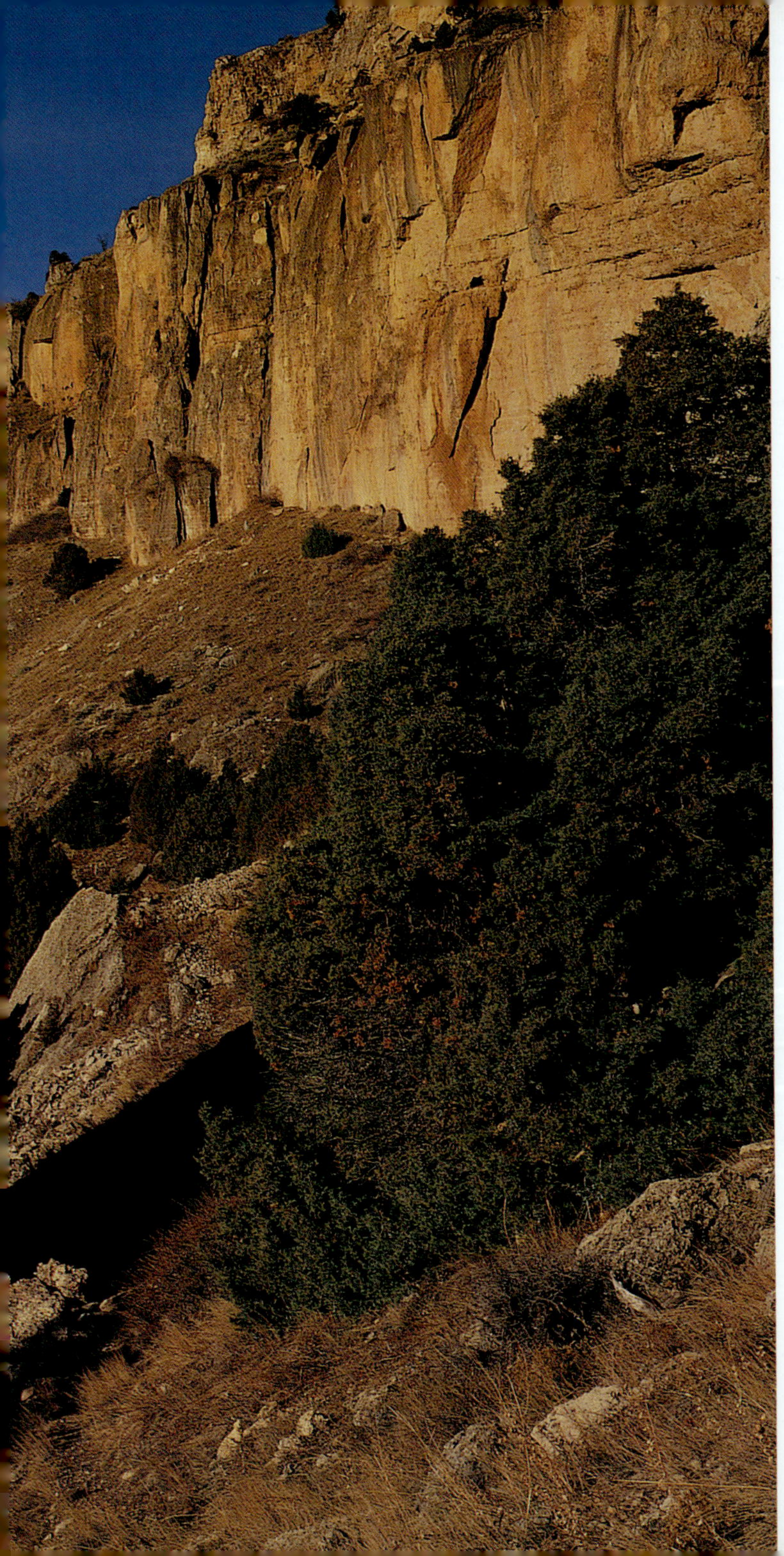

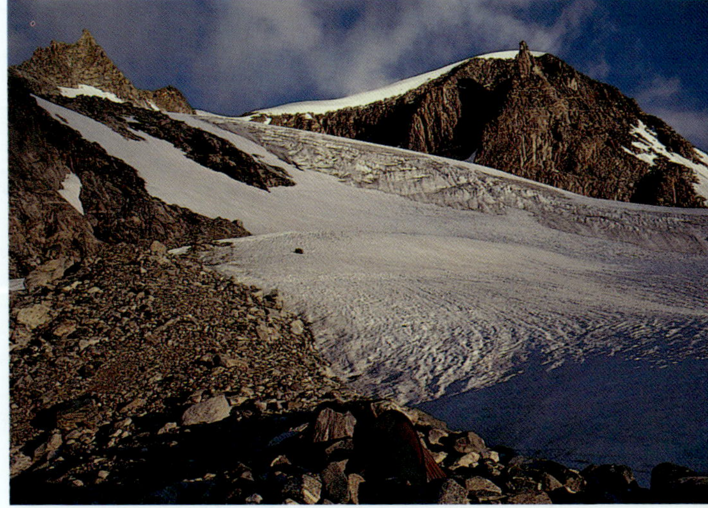

Above: Gooseneck Glacier, one of five glaciers flanking 13,804-foot Gannett Peak, the highest peak in Wyoming.
FRED PFLUGHOFT

Left: Wind River Mountains above rock formations in Sinks Canyon State Park.
FRED PFLUGHOFT

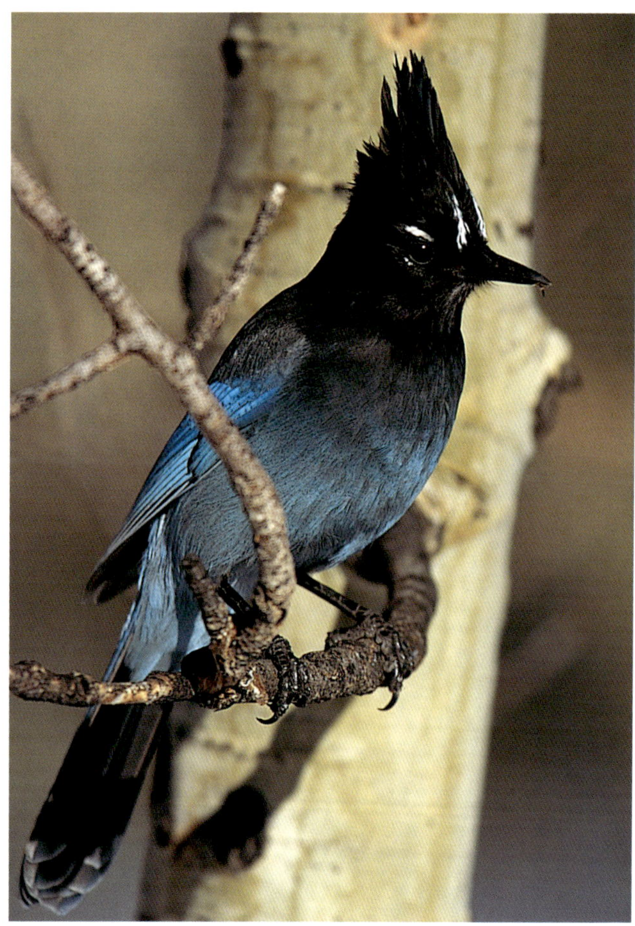

Above: The distinctive Steller's jay; this conspicuous denizen of Wyoming and Montana has the largest range of any North American jay. *ELIZABETH BOEHM*

Right: Mount Lester, located southeast of Island Lake, Bridger Wilderness, is a magnet for electrical storms. *FRED PFLUGHOFT*

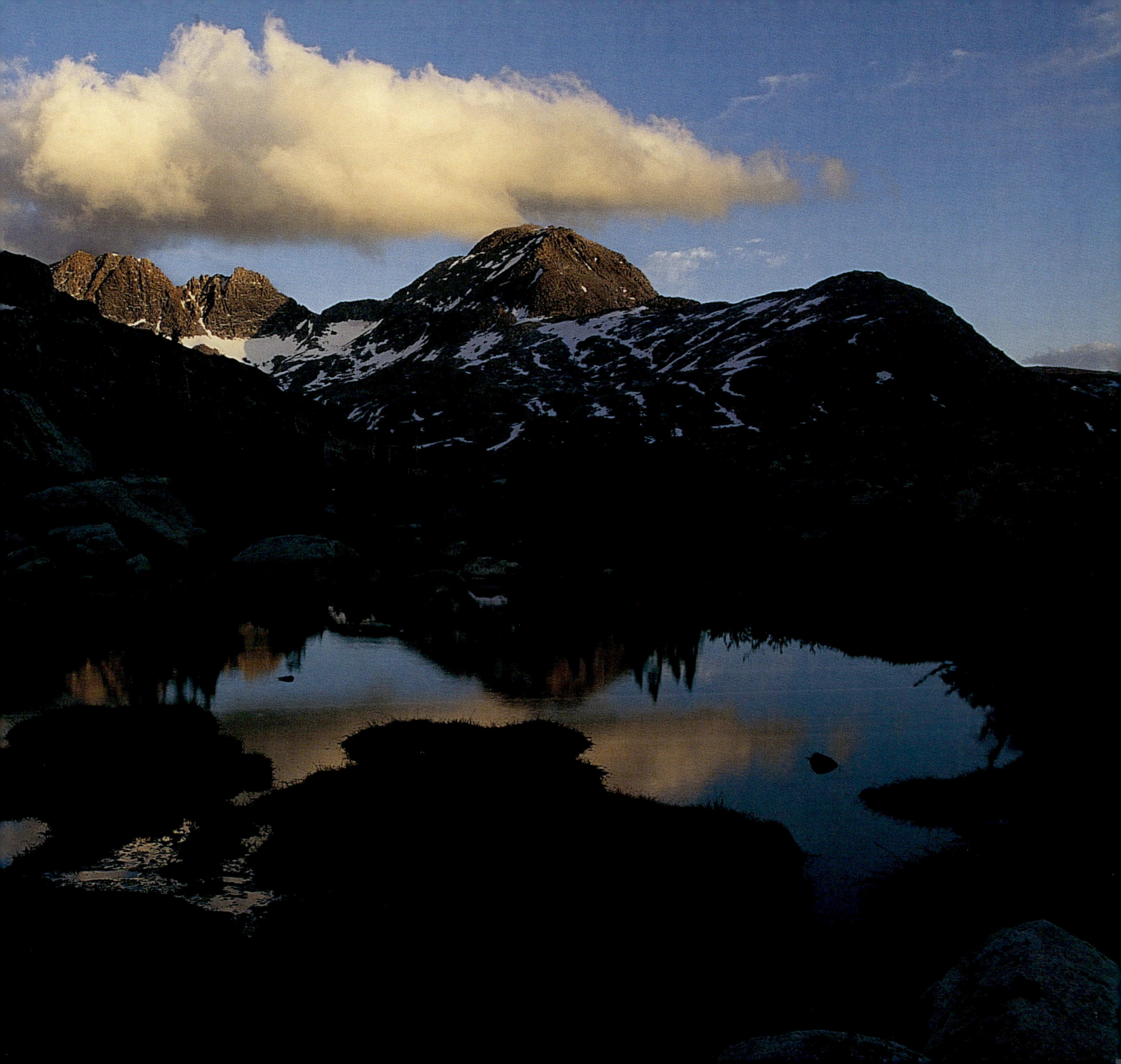

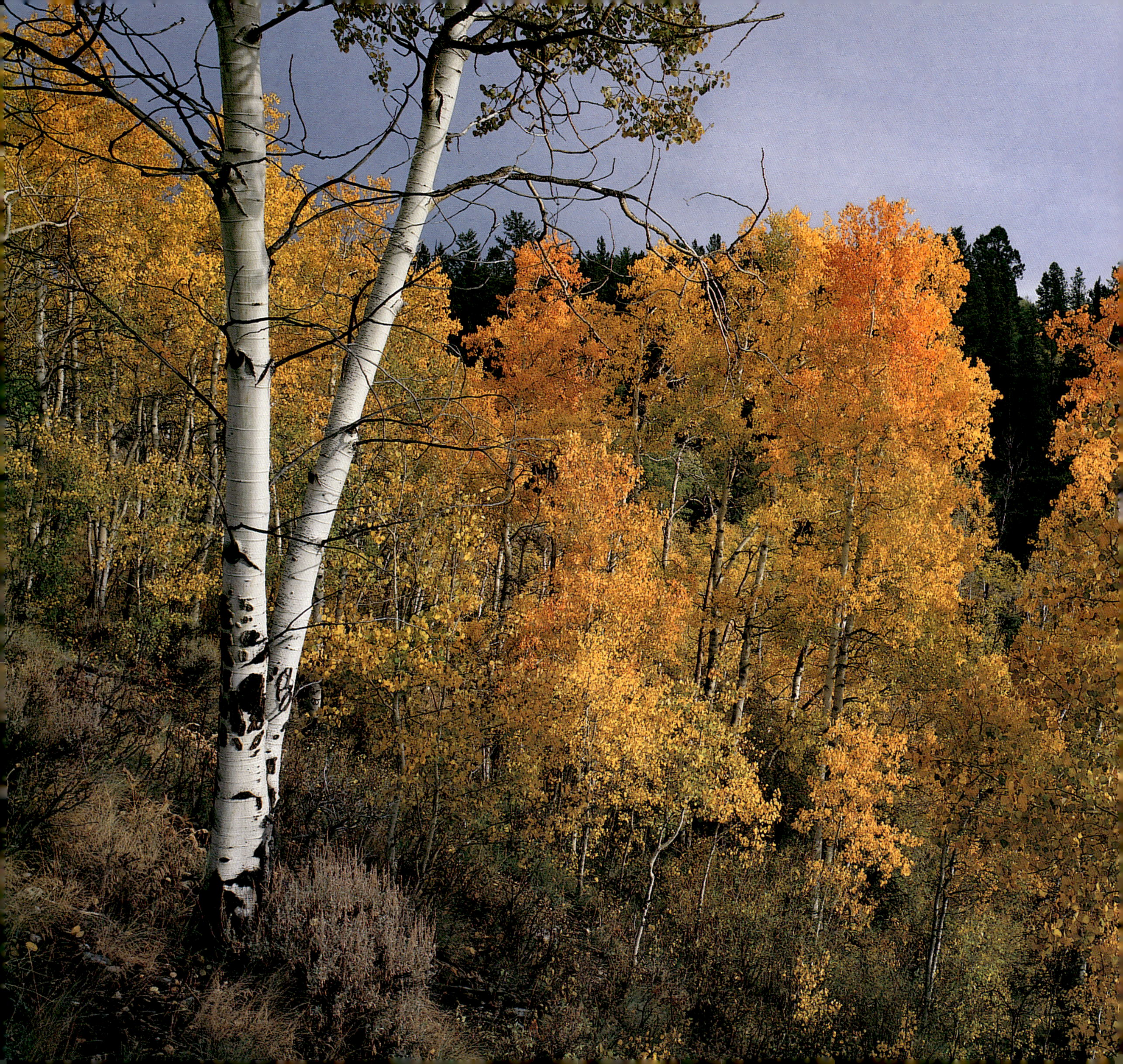

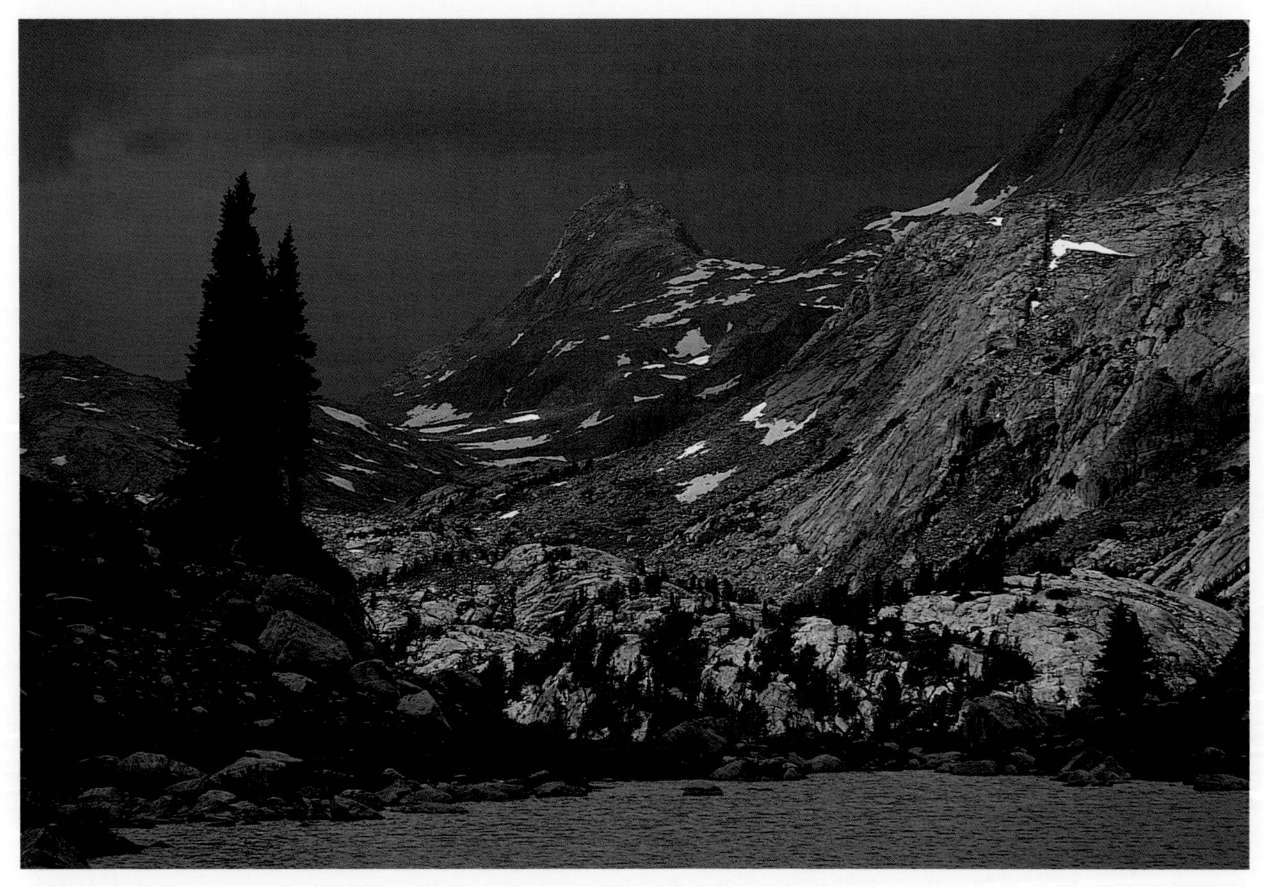

Above: Stroud Peak as seen from Indian Pass Trail.
FRED PFLUGHOFT

Facing page: Aspens in fall splendor, Bridger-Teton National Forest.
FRED PFLUGHOFT

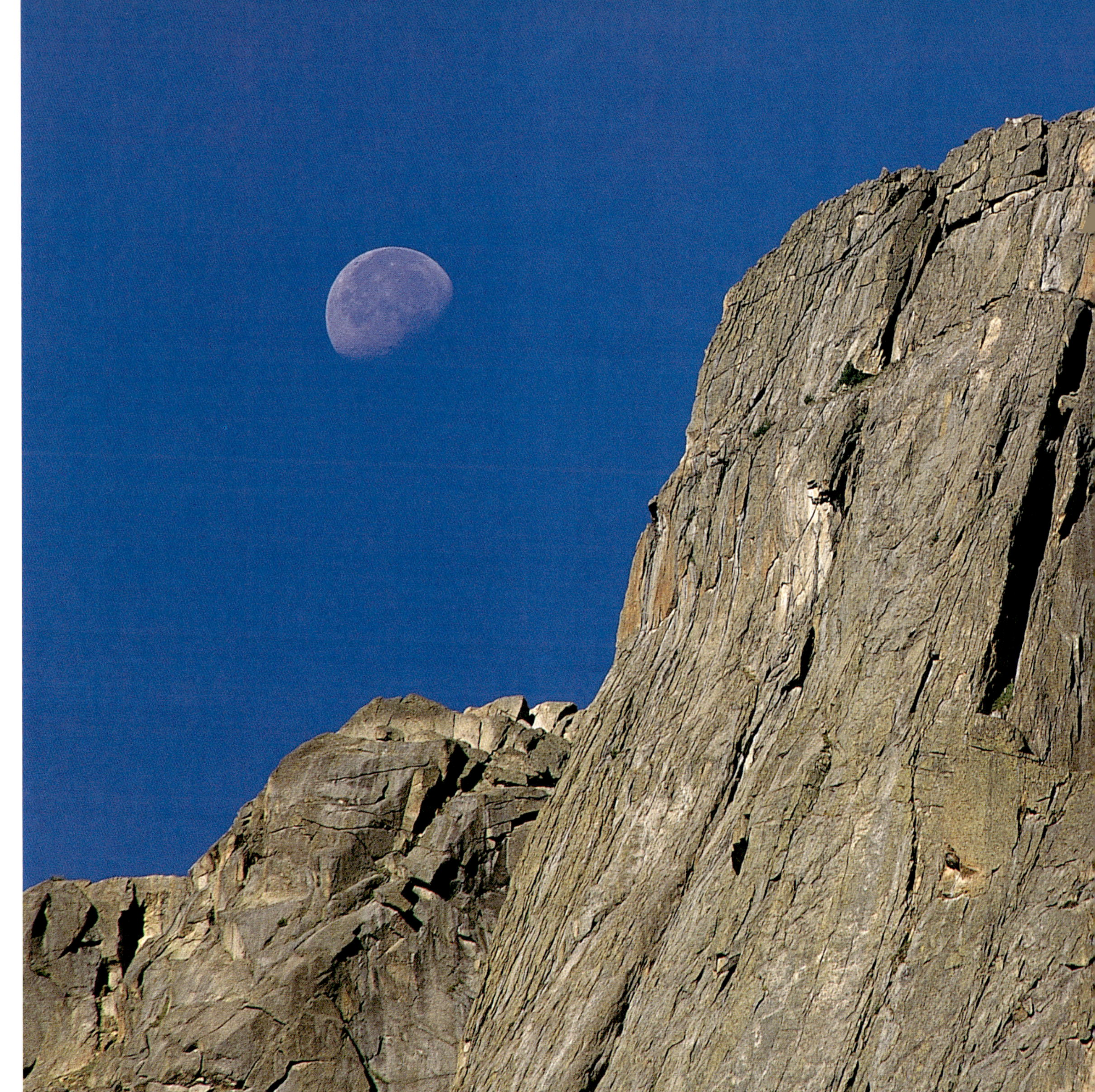

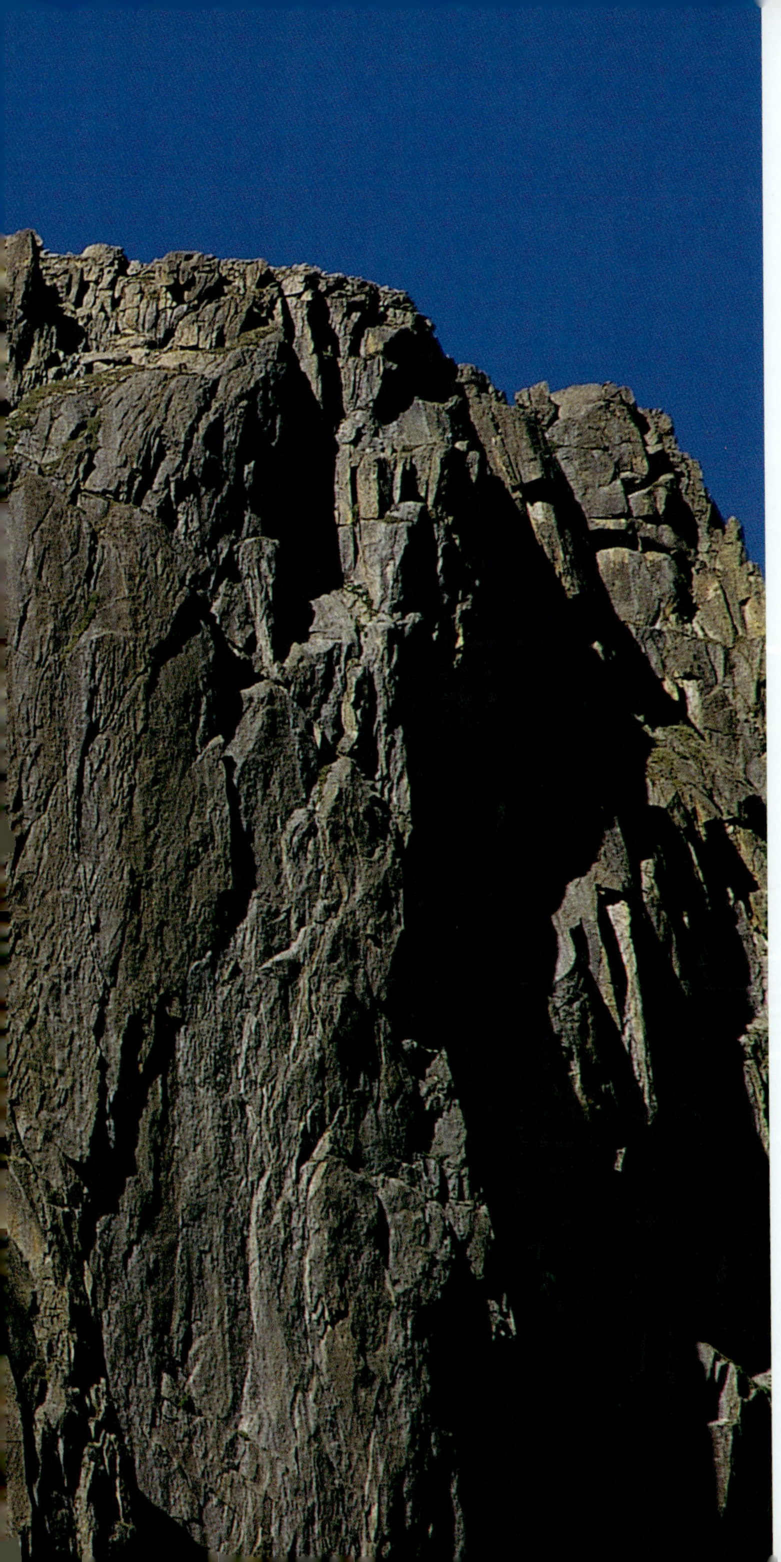

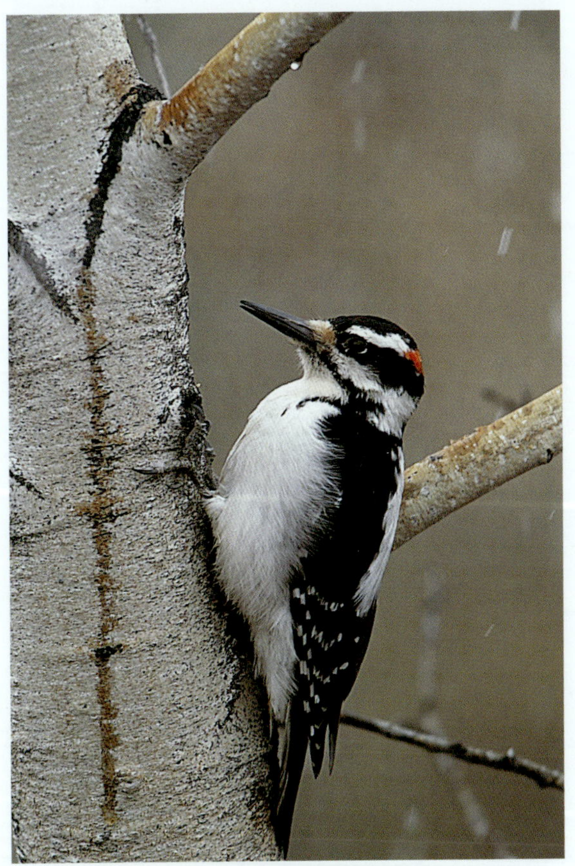

Above: Hairy woodpeckers can be distinguished from other species by their white backs and large bills. Males can be identified by the red spot at the back of the head.
ELIZABETH BOEHM

Left: Moon over Dome Peak from New Fork Park.
FRED PFLUGHOFT

Following pages: Titcomb Needles reflected at sunrise.
FRED PFLUGHOFT

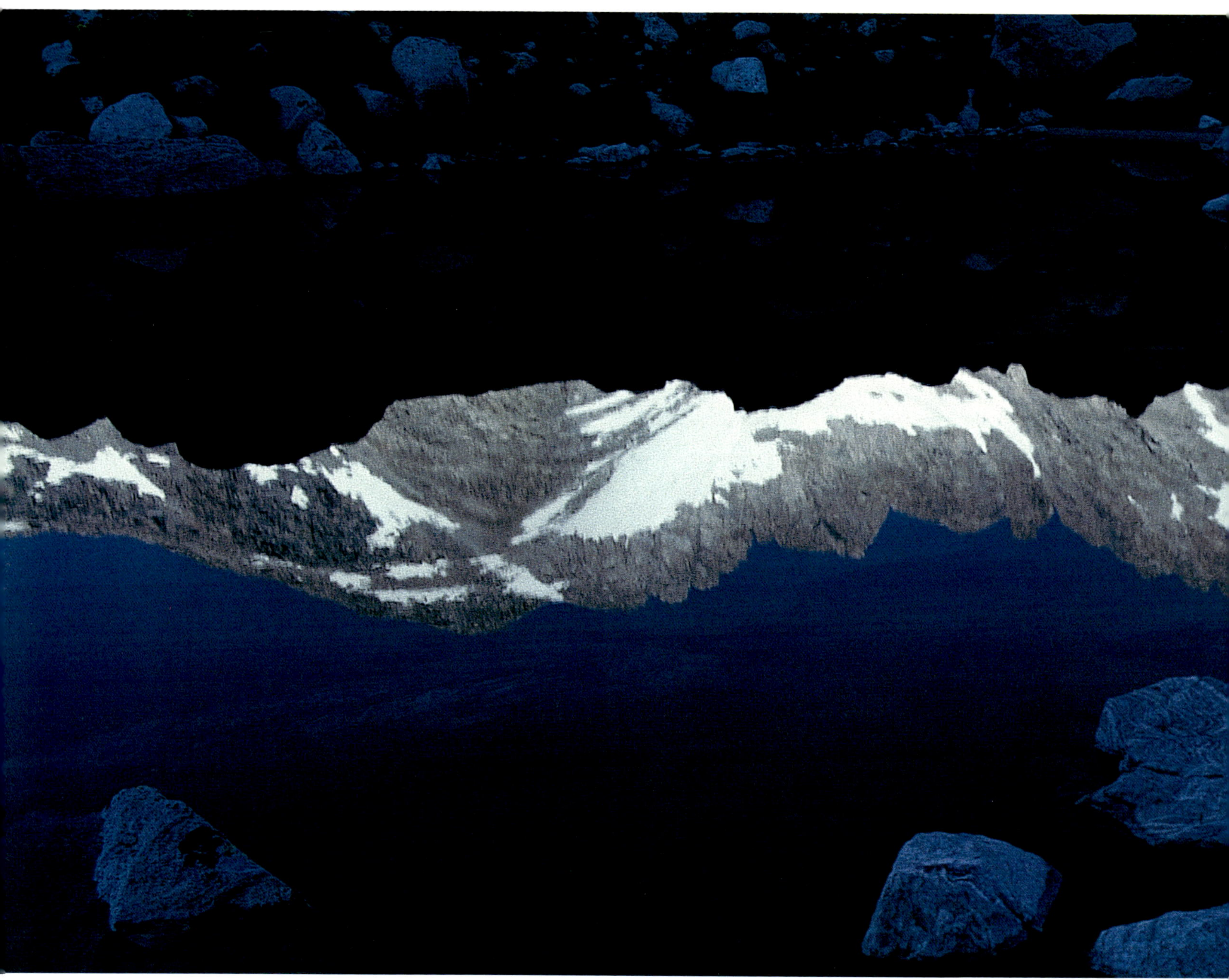

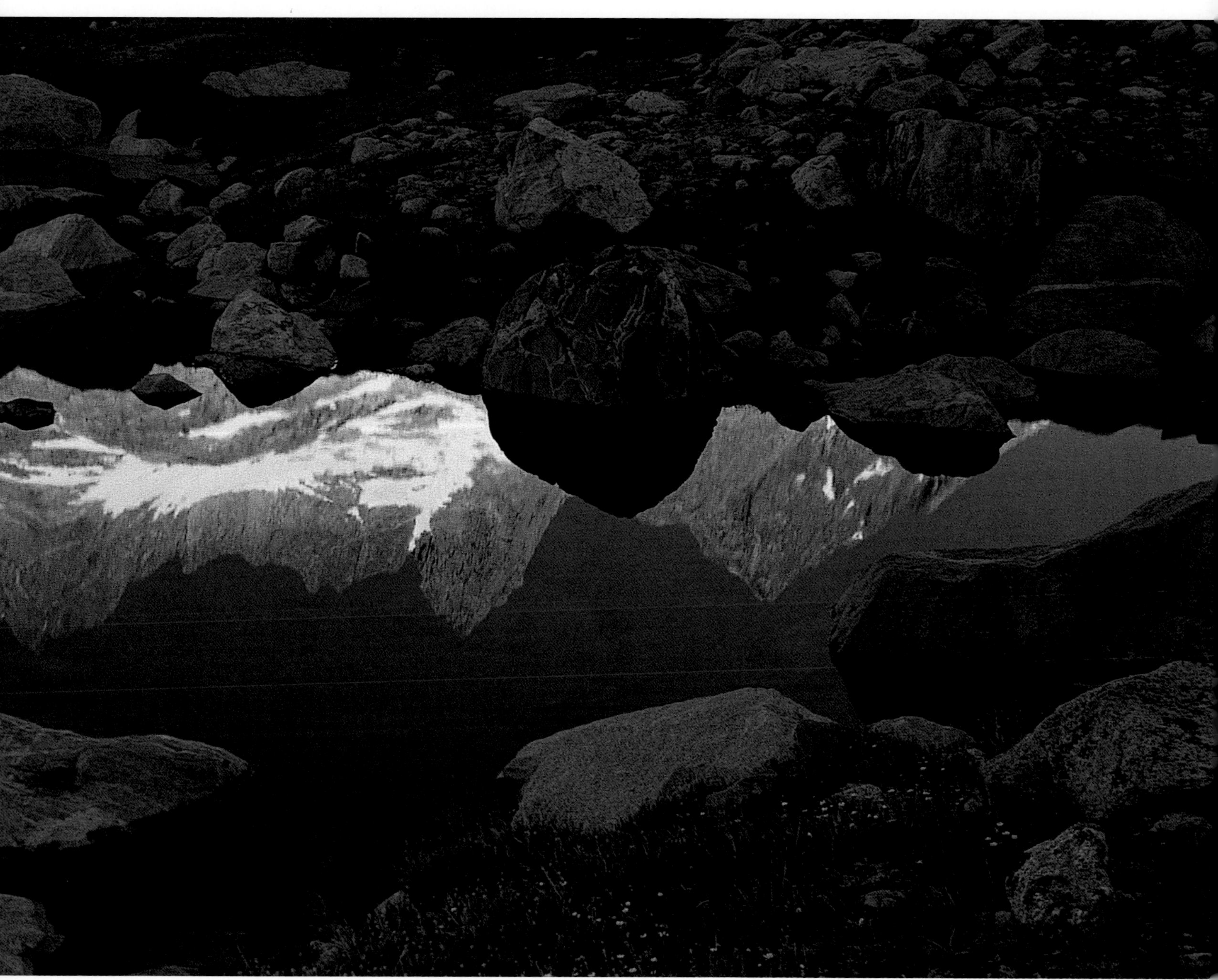

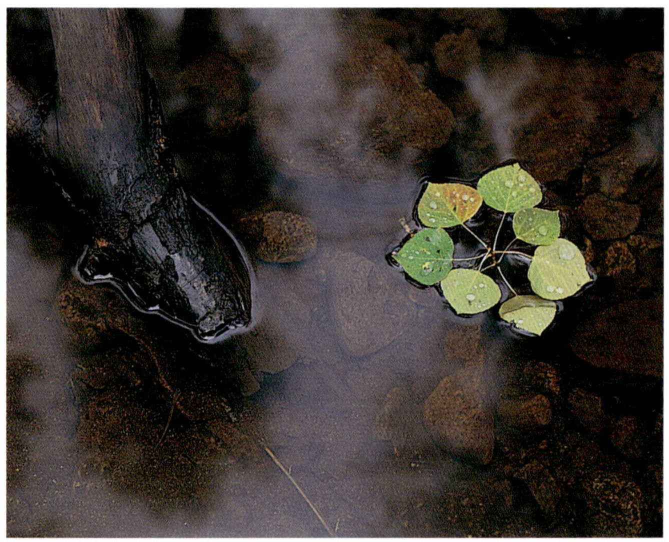

Above: Aspen leaves afloat in a mountain creek.
DELSA SMITH ALLEN

Right: Lake Isabella, with Medina Mountain in the distance, Bridger Wilderness. *DELSA SMITH ALLEN*

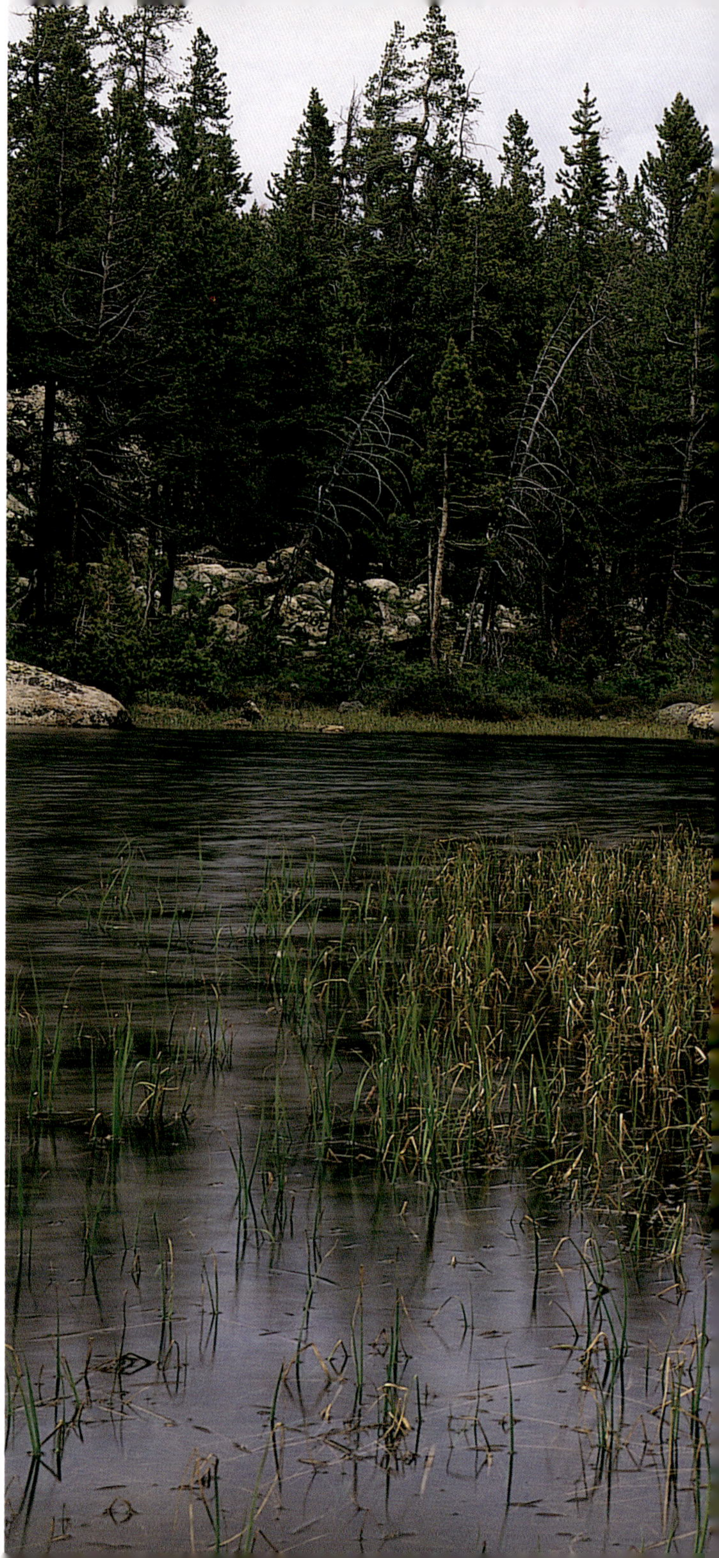

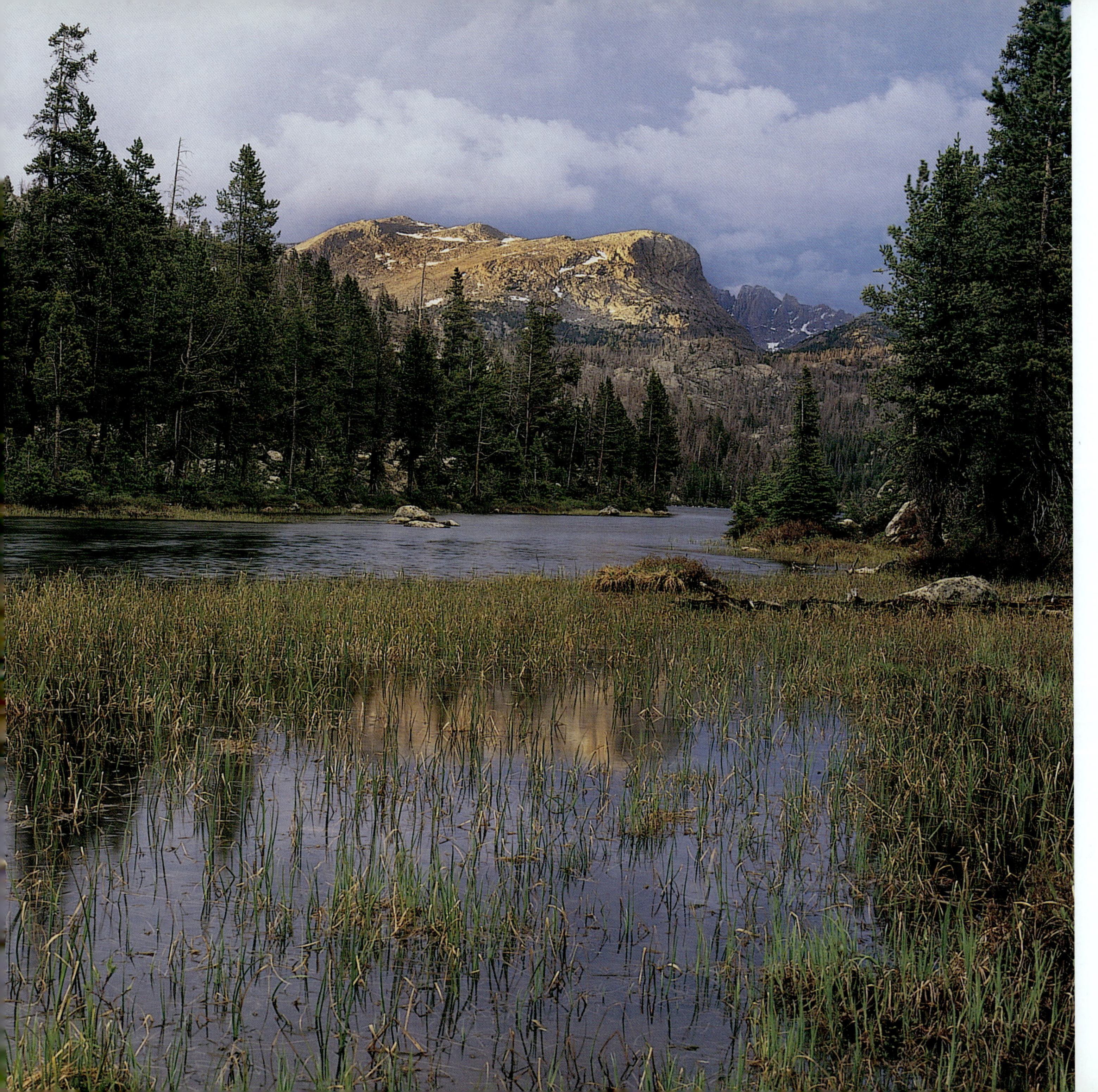

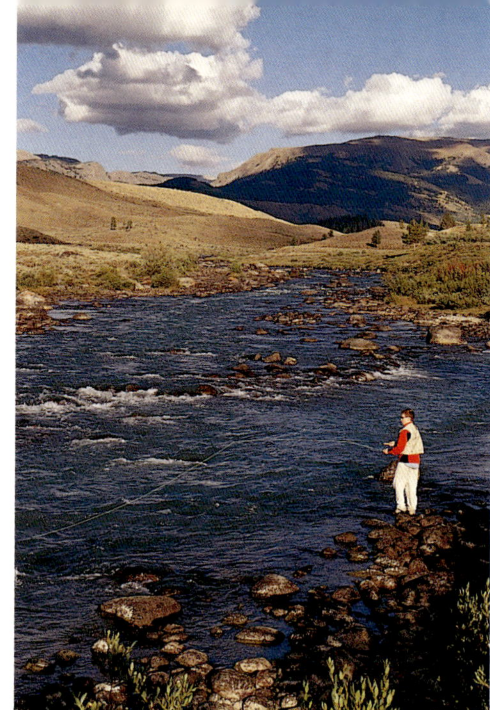

Right: Flyfishing on the Upper Green River, which is fed by streams flowing from atop the Continental Divide.
FRED PFLUGHOFT

Facing page: The conspicuous profile of Flat Top Mountain, Bridger Wilderness.
FRED PFLUGHOFT

Below: High camp beneath American Legion Peak.
FRED PFLUGHOFT

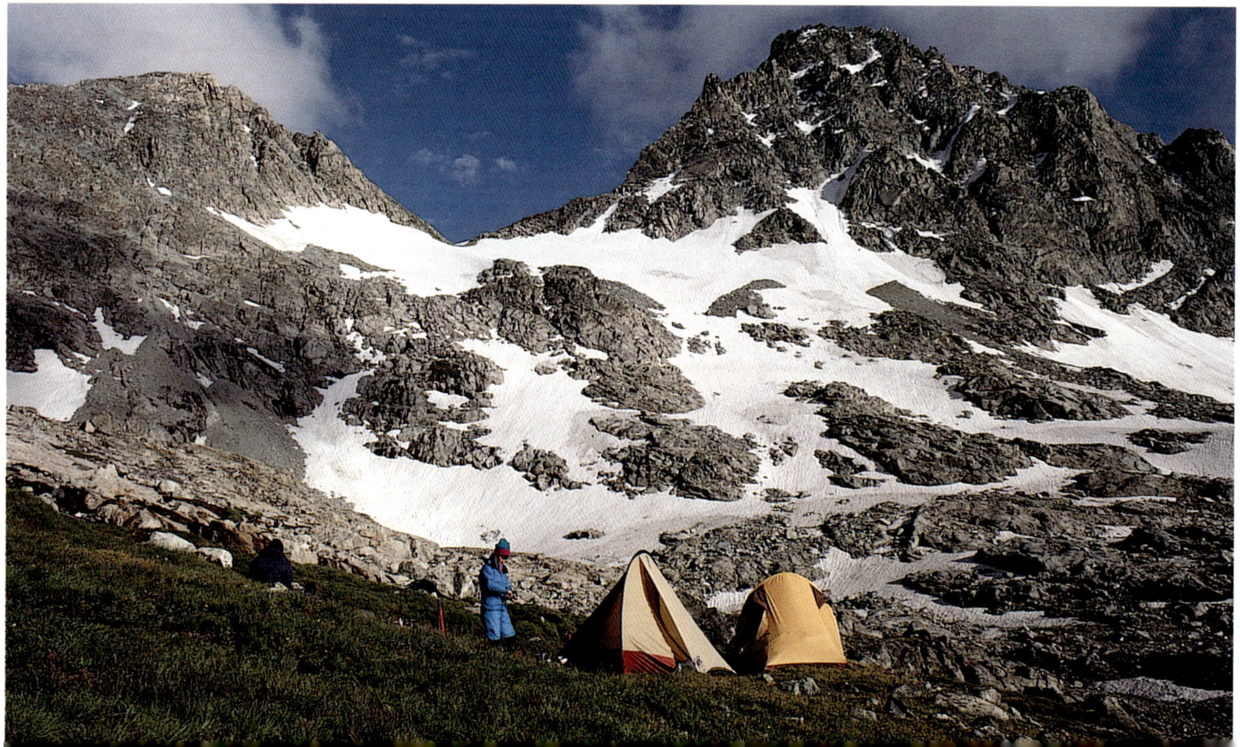

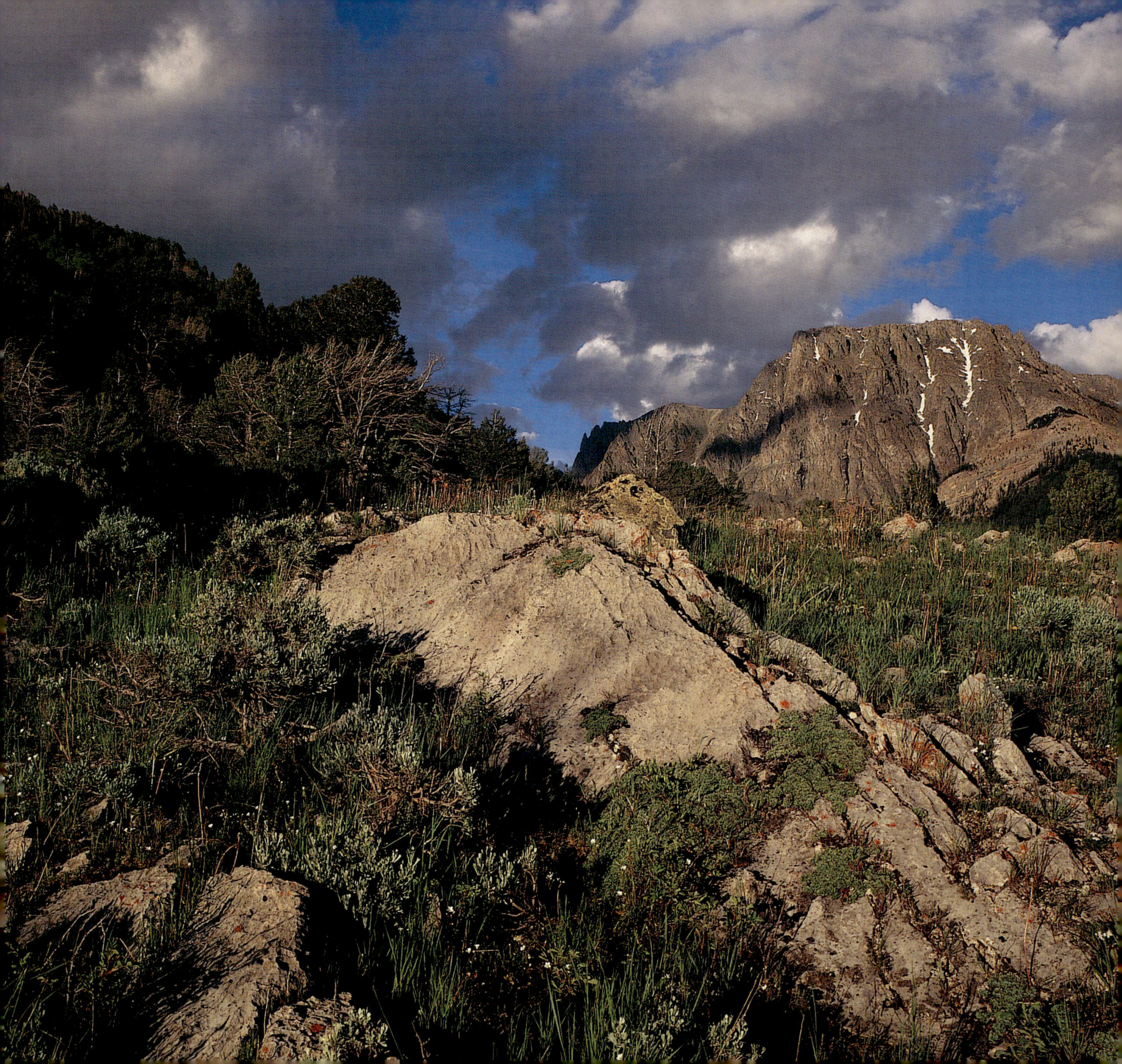

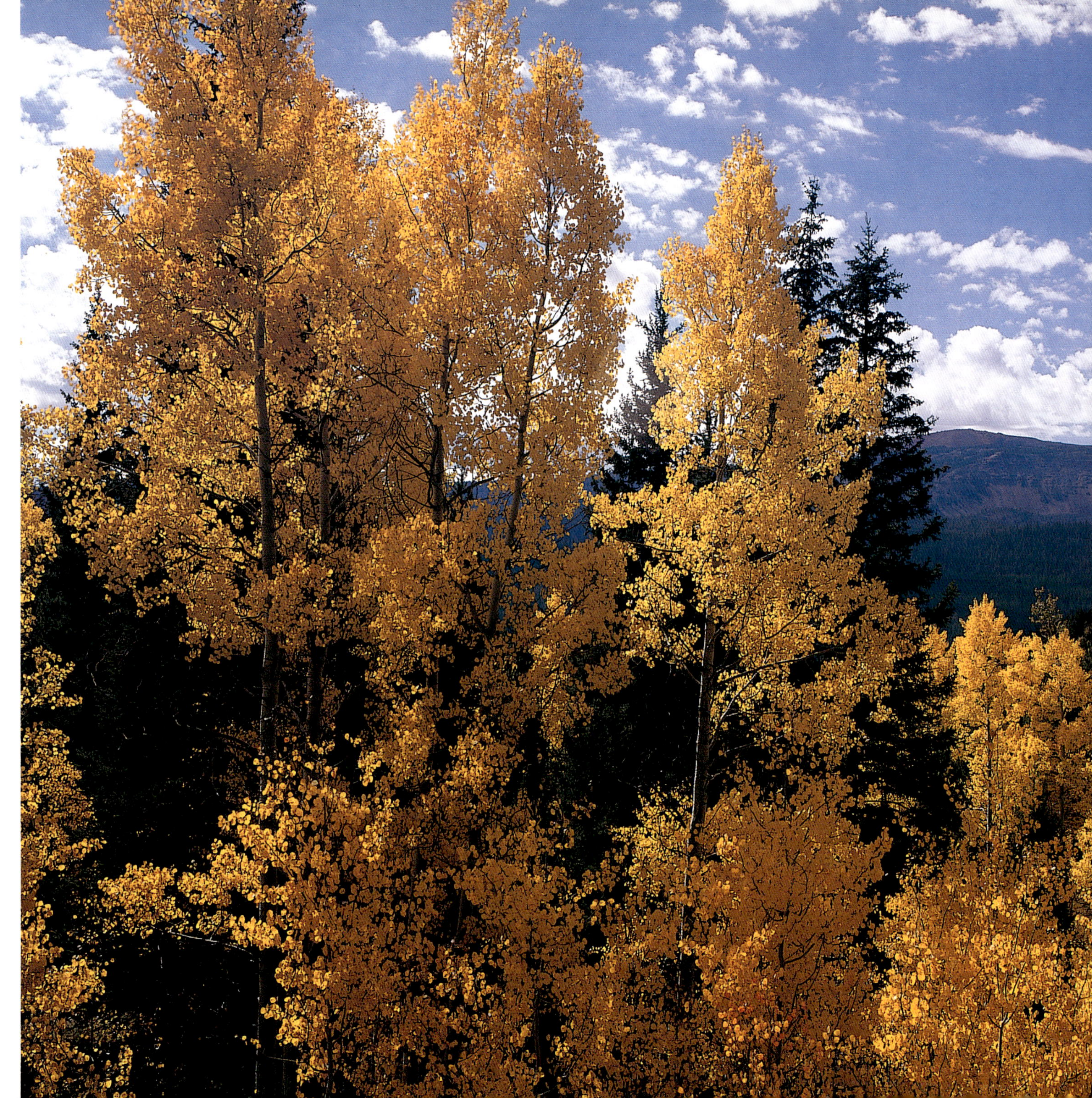

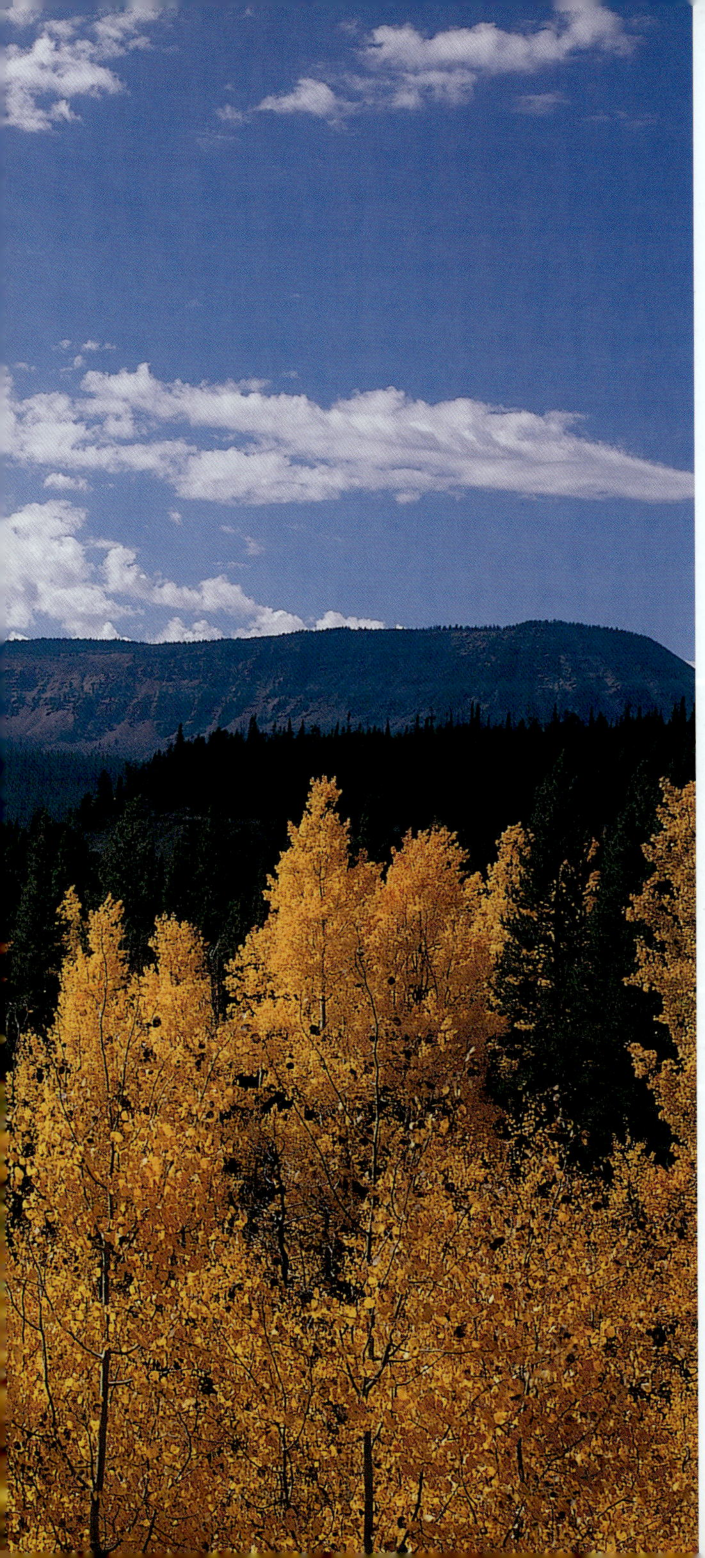

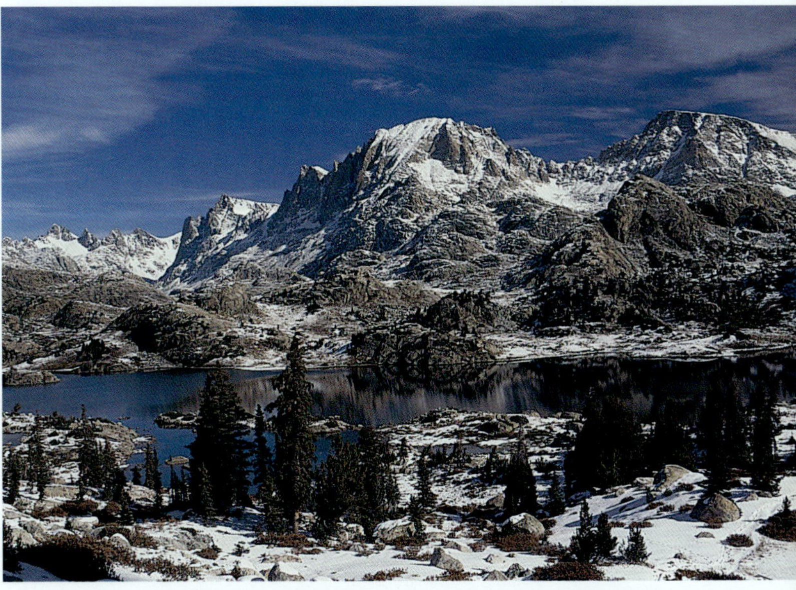

Above: Autumn snowfall at Island Lake, Fremont and Jackson peaks.
BEN FRANKLIN

Left: Lava Mountain, northern terminus of the Wind River Range.
FRED PFLUGHOFT

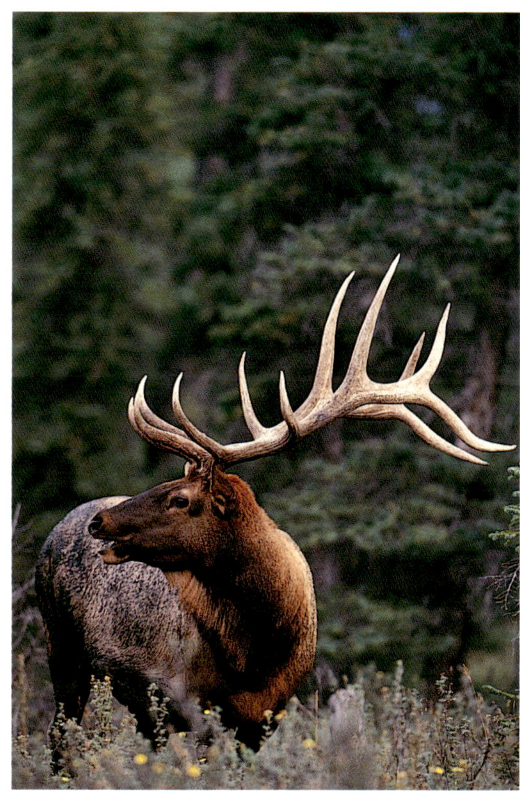

Above: Bull elk. Bulls weigh between 500 and 800 pounds. *JOHN L. HINDERMAN*

Right: 12,254-foot Mount Victor overlooks Upper Pipestone Lakes, Bridger Wilderness. *DELSA SMITH ALLEN*

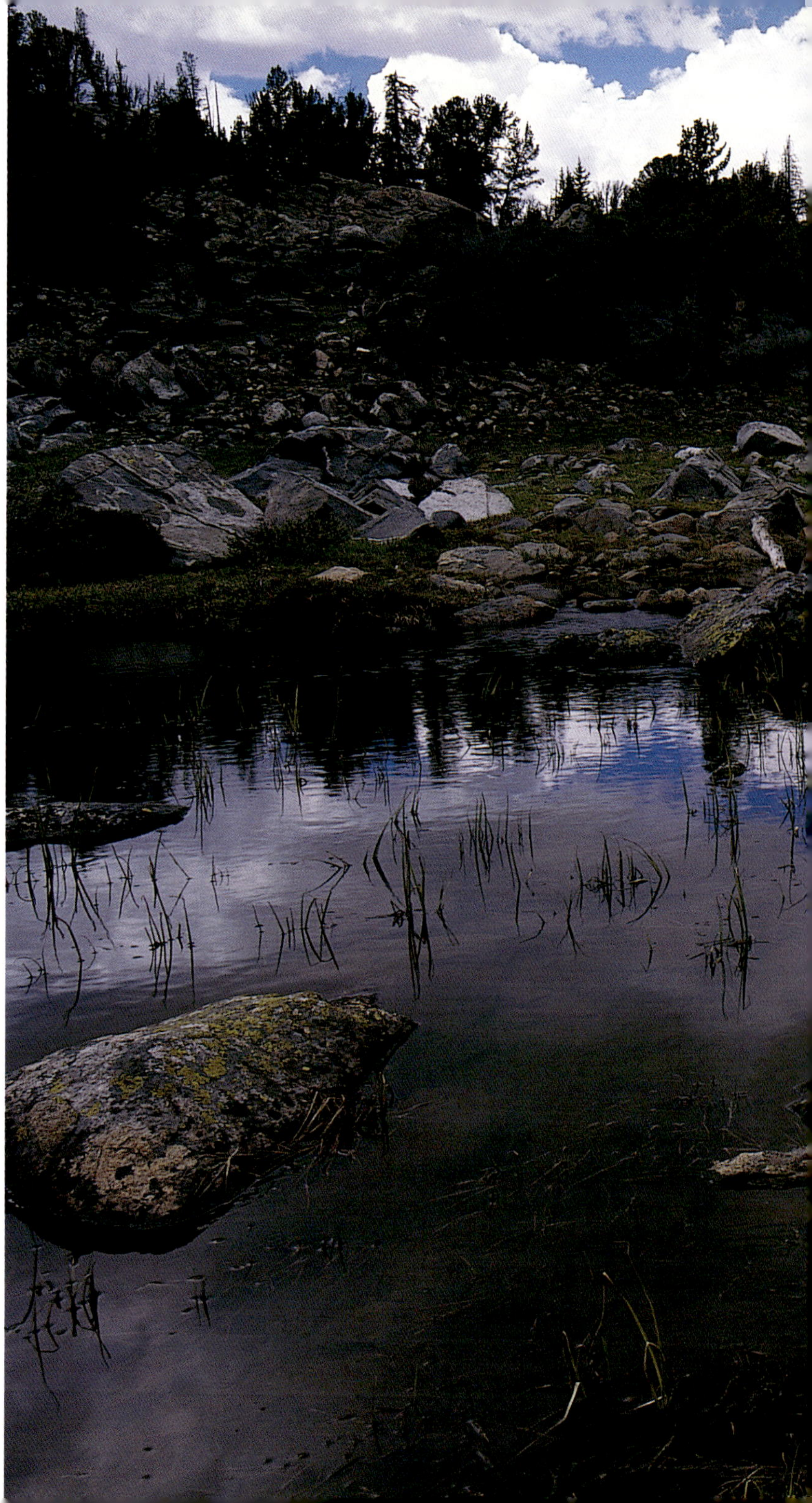

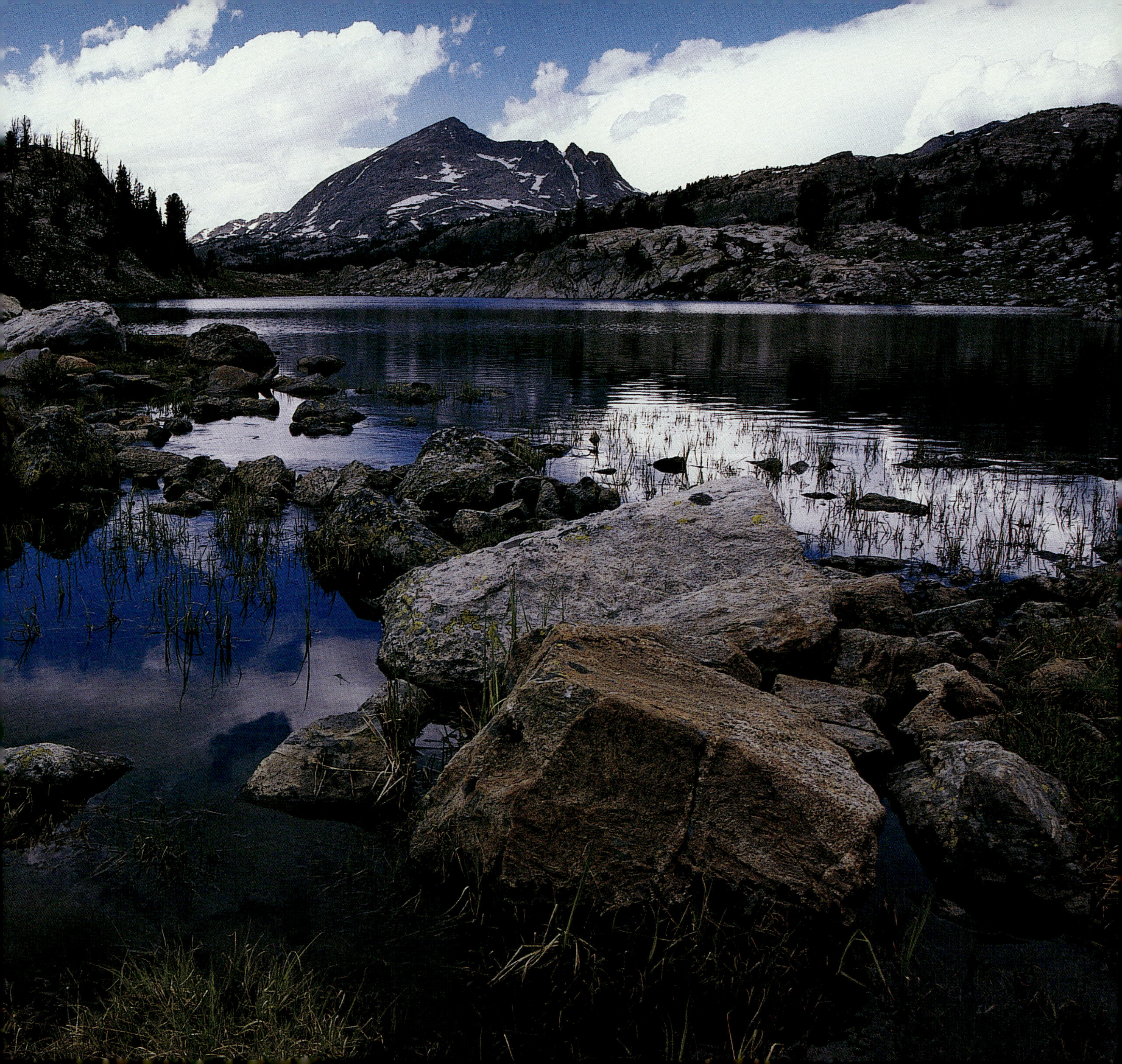

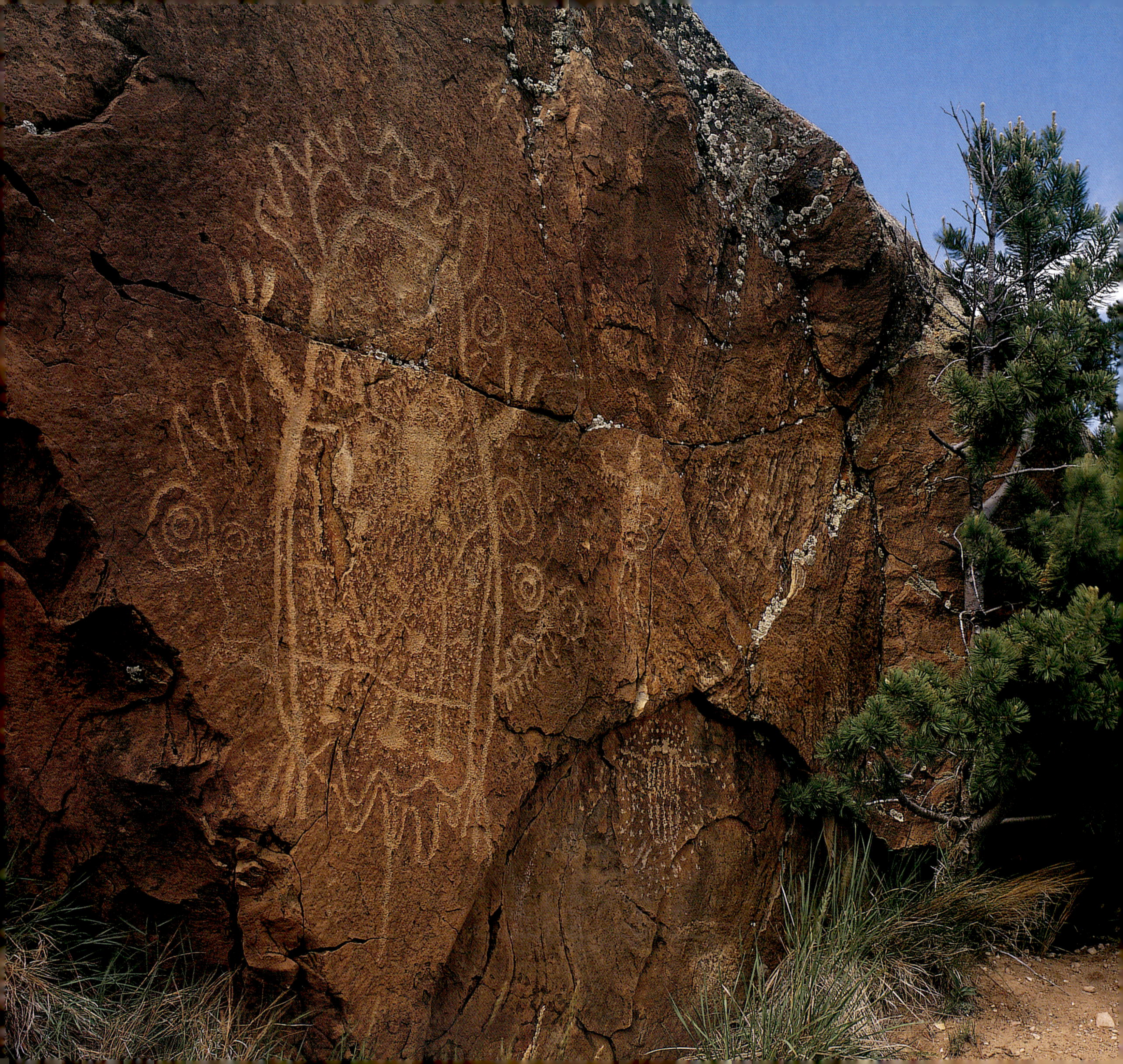

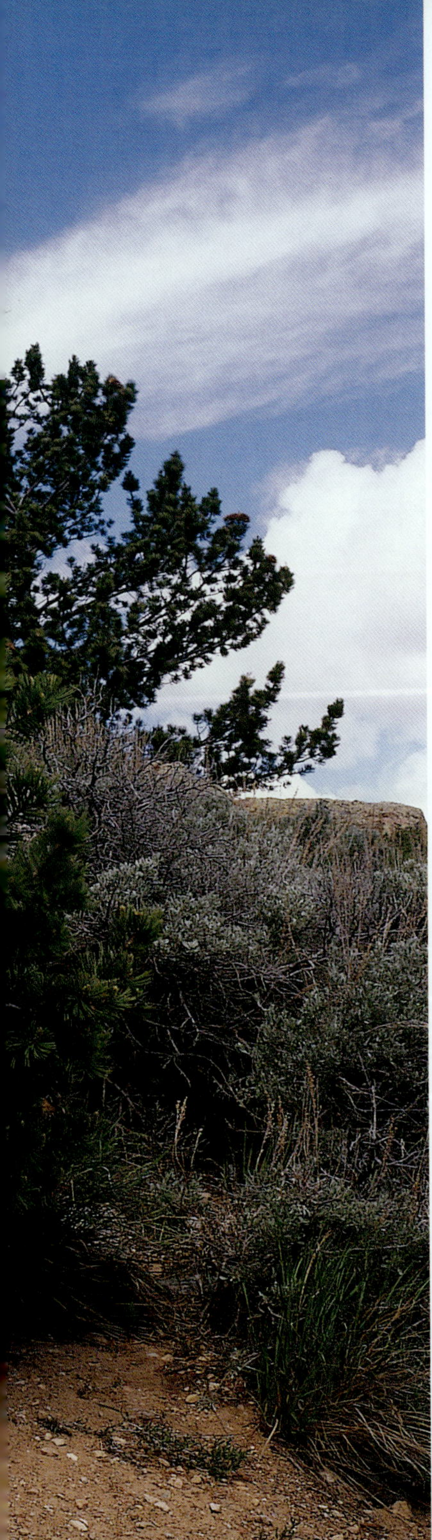

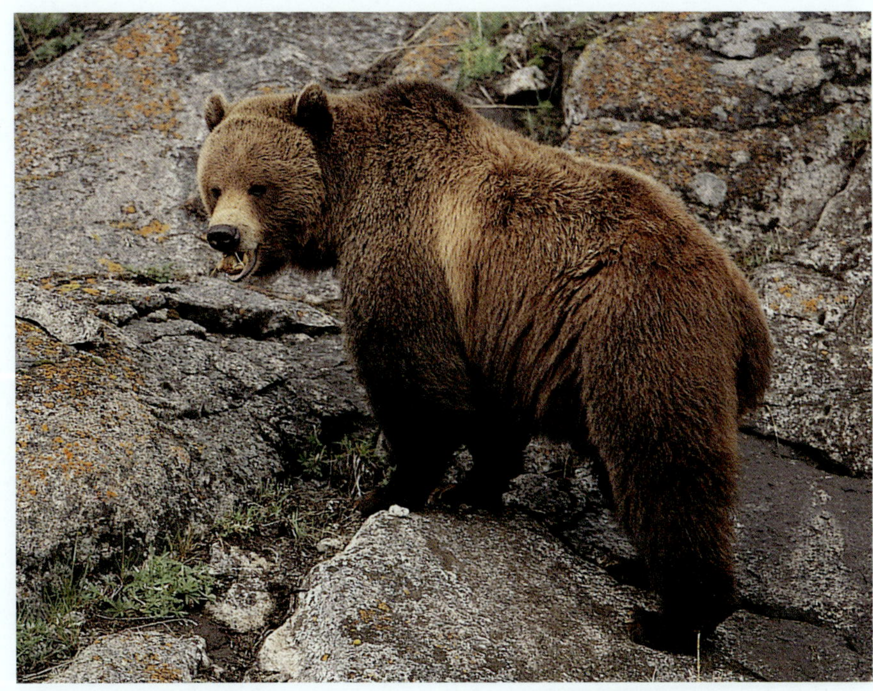

Above: Grizzly bears have reestablished themselves throughout the Greater Yellowstone Ecosystem and are now seen, although infrequently, in the northern portions of the Wind River Range. *JOHN C. ERIKSSON*

Left: Petroglyphs located in a 3-mile-long grouping of rock art near Torrey Lakes, Shoshone National Forest. *FRED PFLUGHOFT*

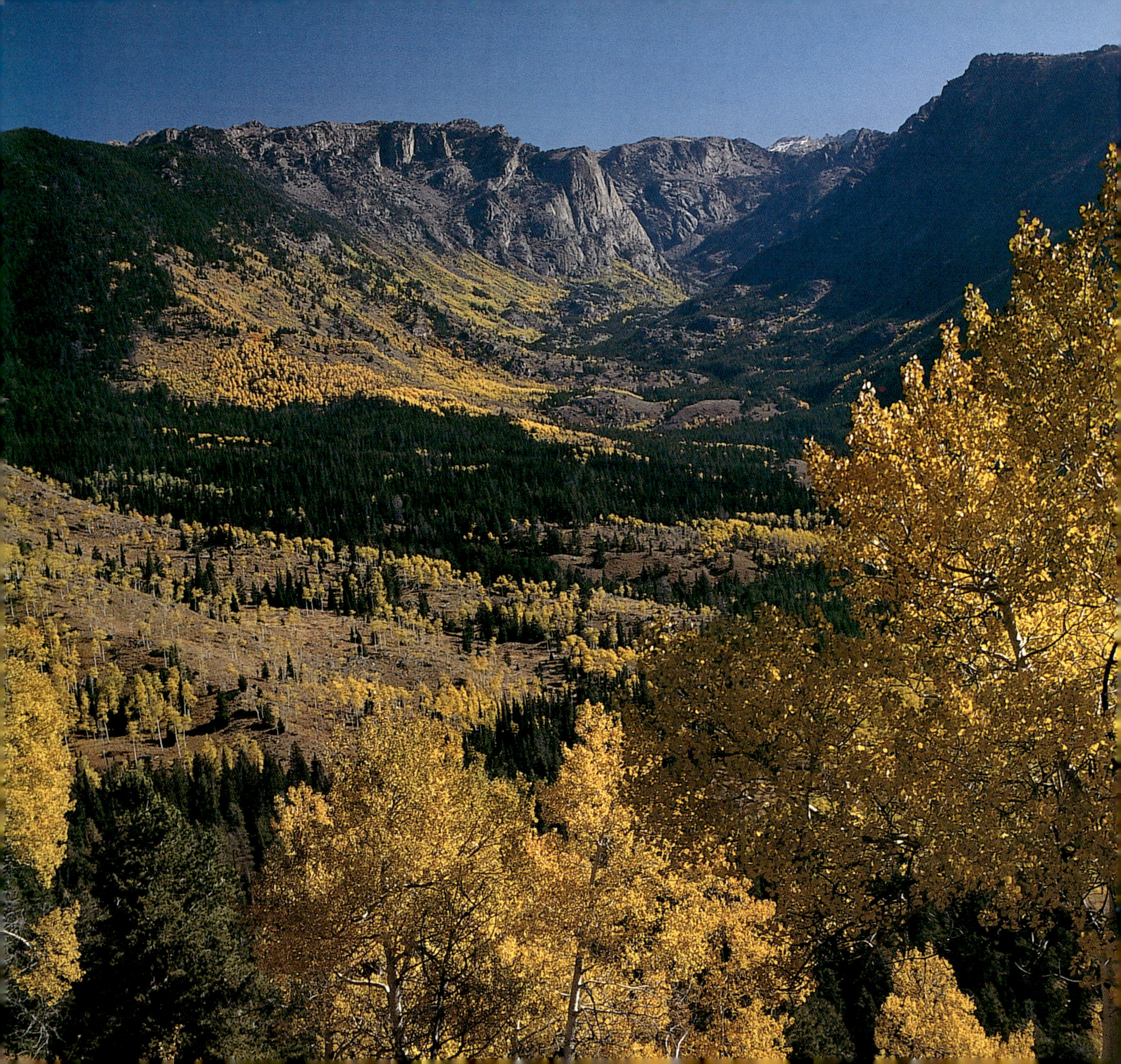

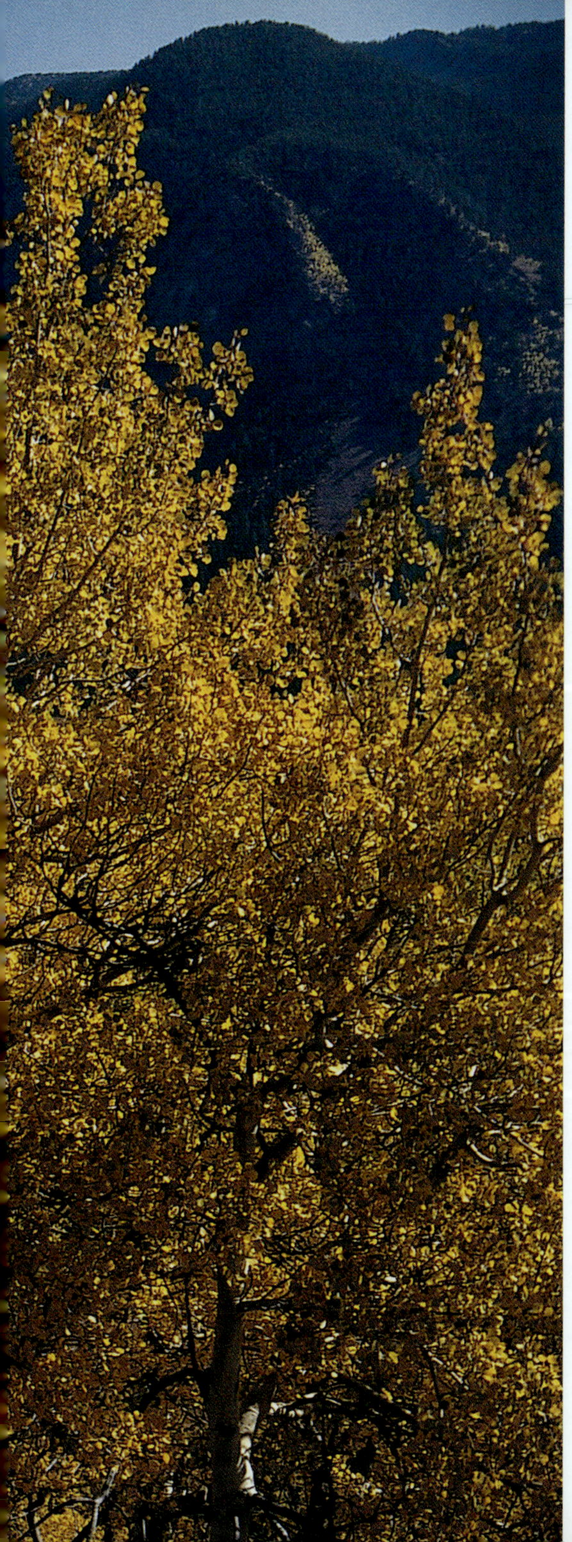

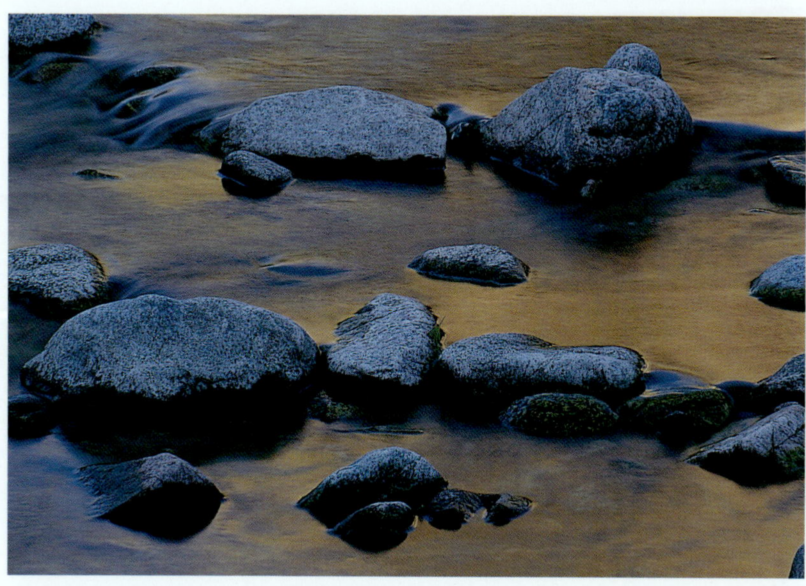

Above: Evening reflections in the New Fork River at New Fork Park, Bridger Wilderness.
FRED PFLUGHOFT

Left: Fall arrives in New Fork Canyon, a glacially carved valley that opens to the prairie, Bridger-Teton National Forest.
BEN FRANKLIN

Following pages: View of Haystack Mountain and East Temple and Temple peaks from Jackass Pass Trail. *FRED PFLUGHOFT*

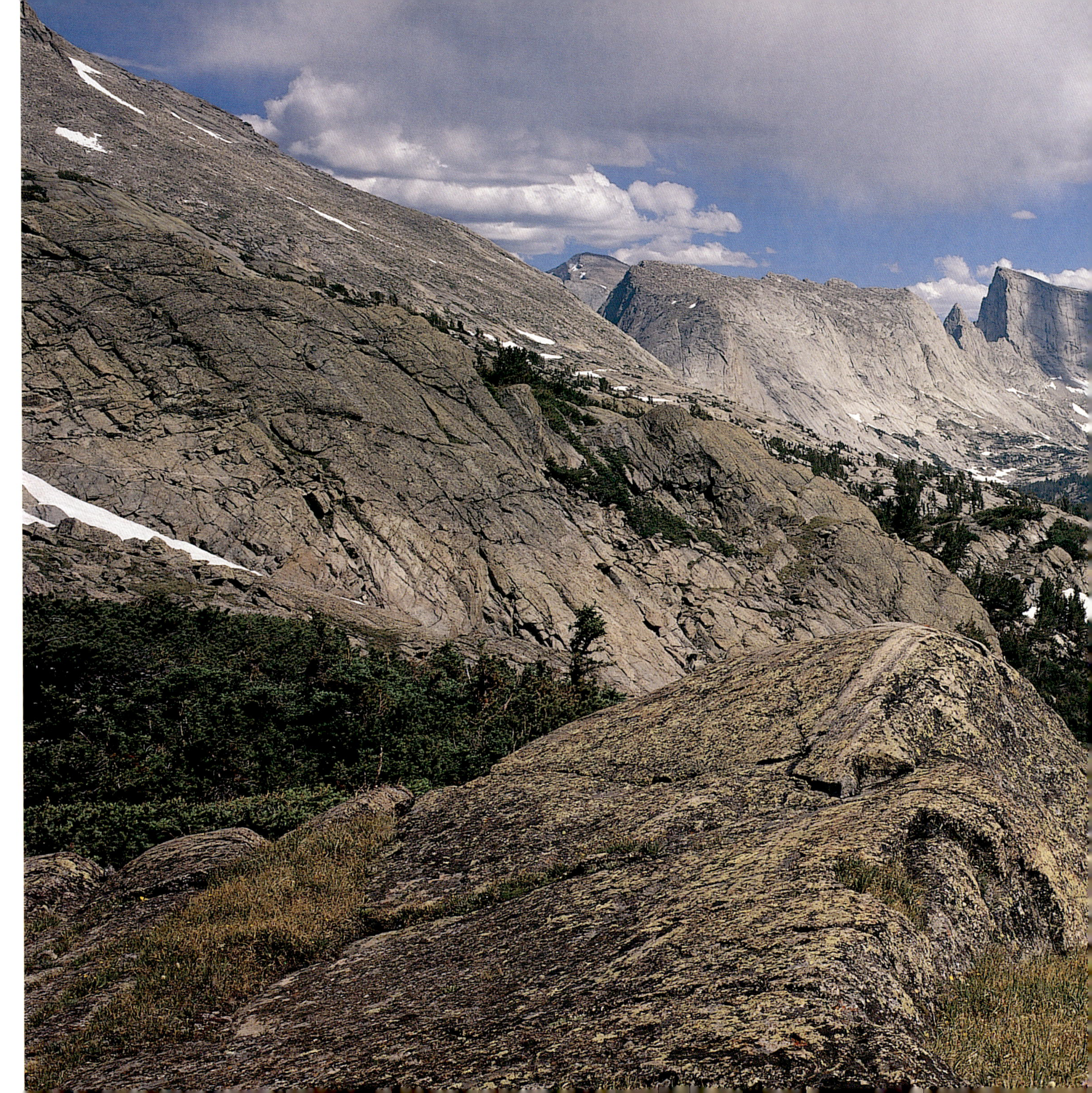

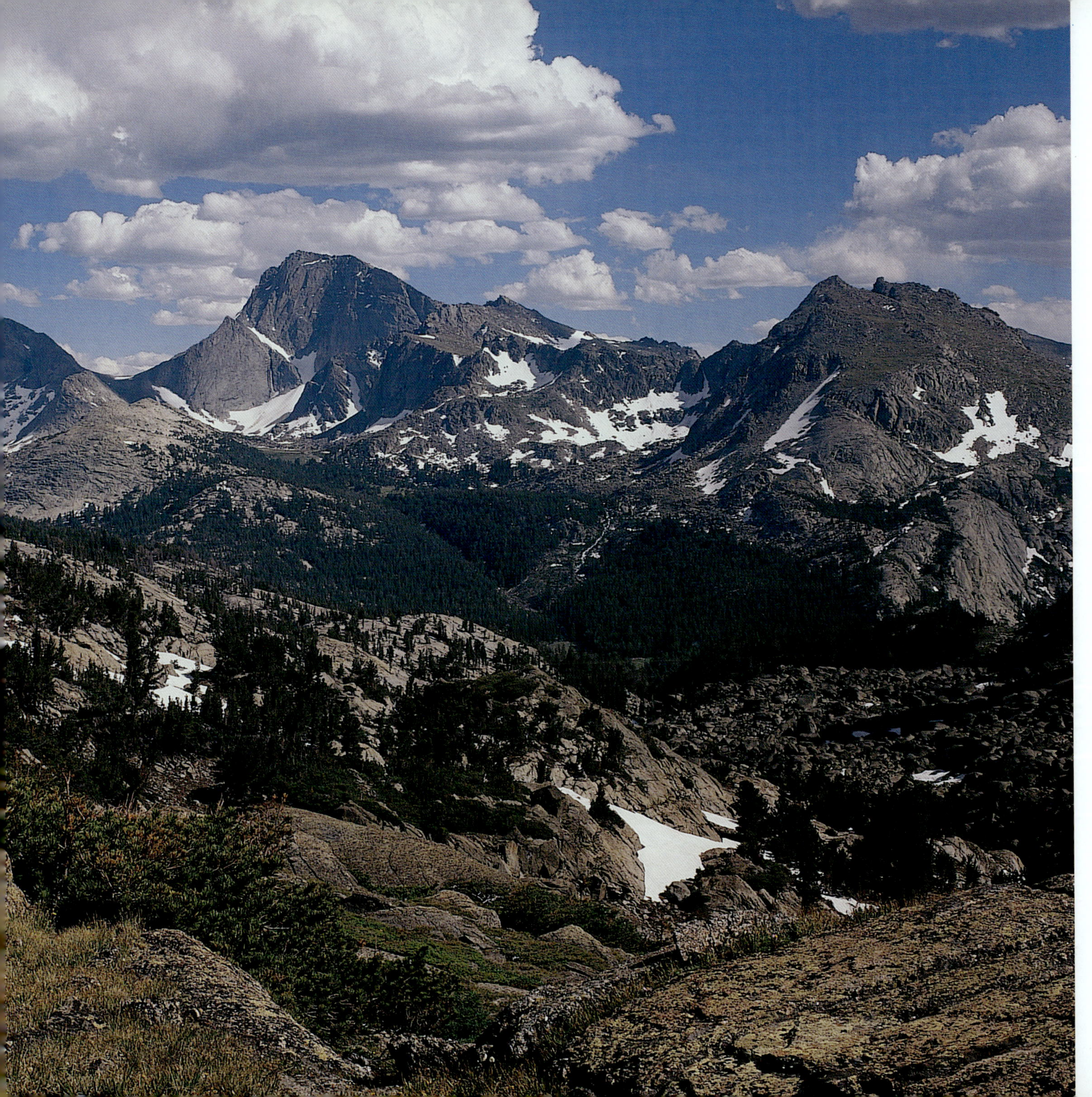

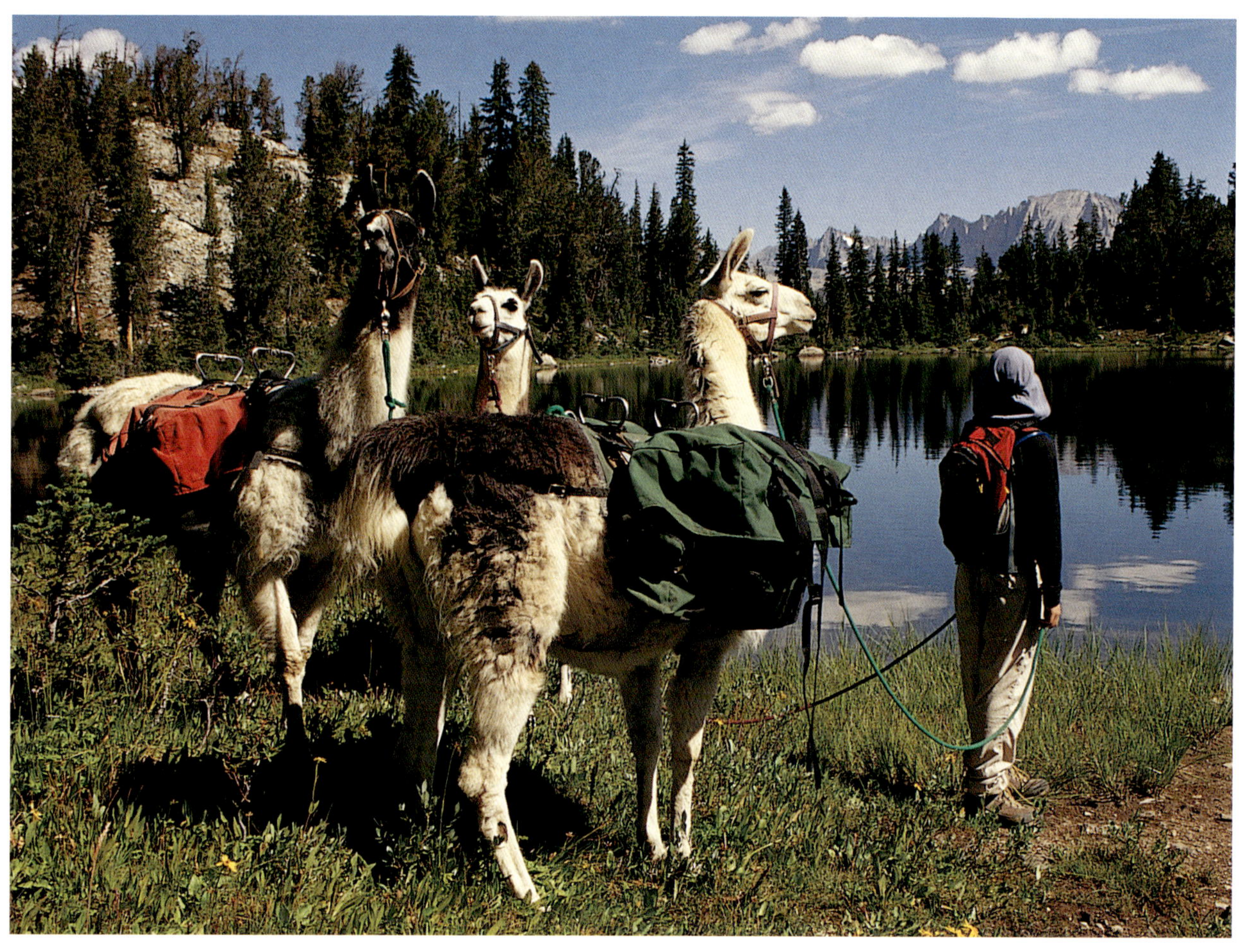

Above: Llama packing, Barbara Lake. FRED PFLUGHOFT

Facing page: Left of center is "The Bottle" as seen from the summit ridge of Squaretop Mountain. FRED PFLUGHOFT

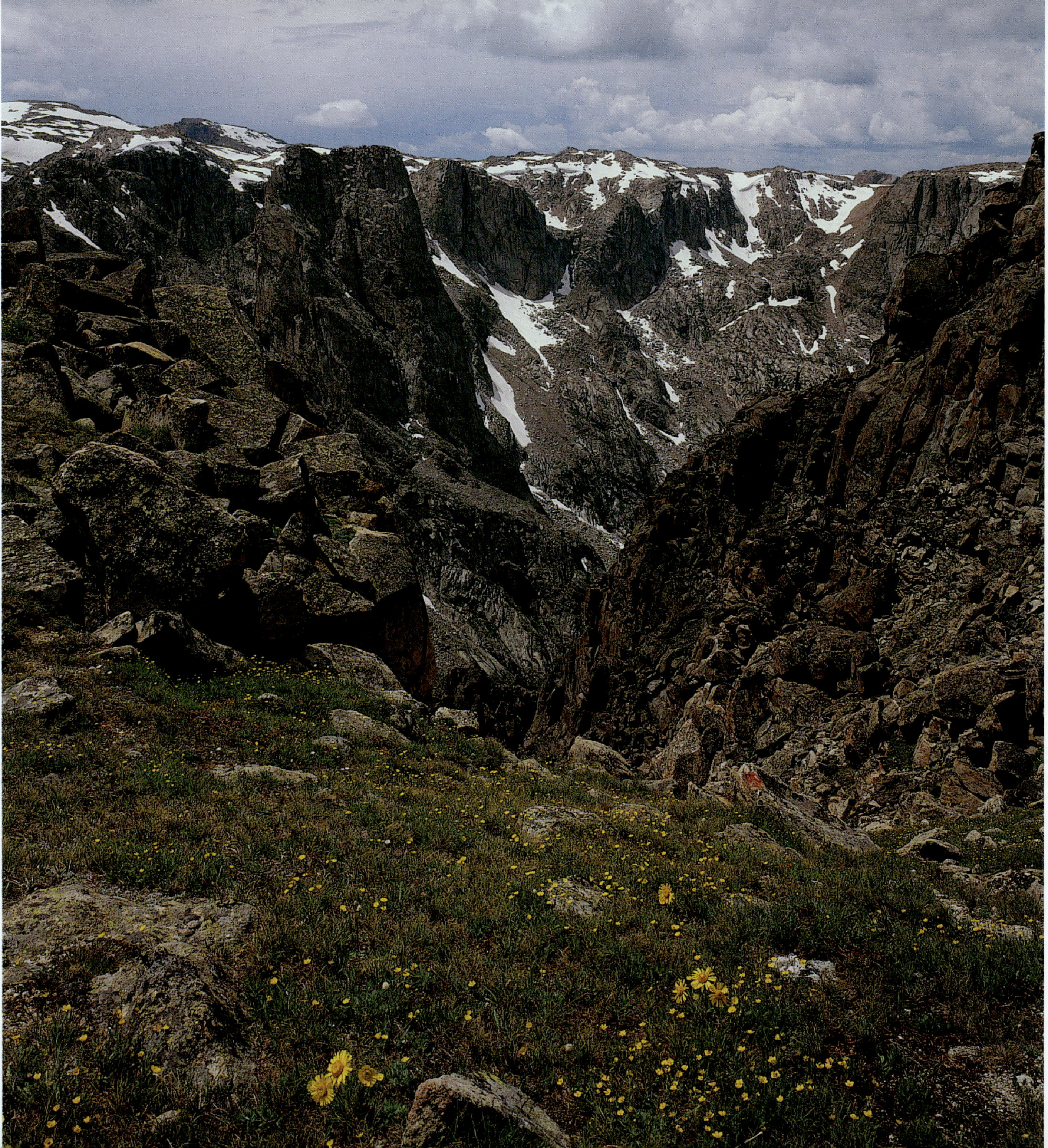

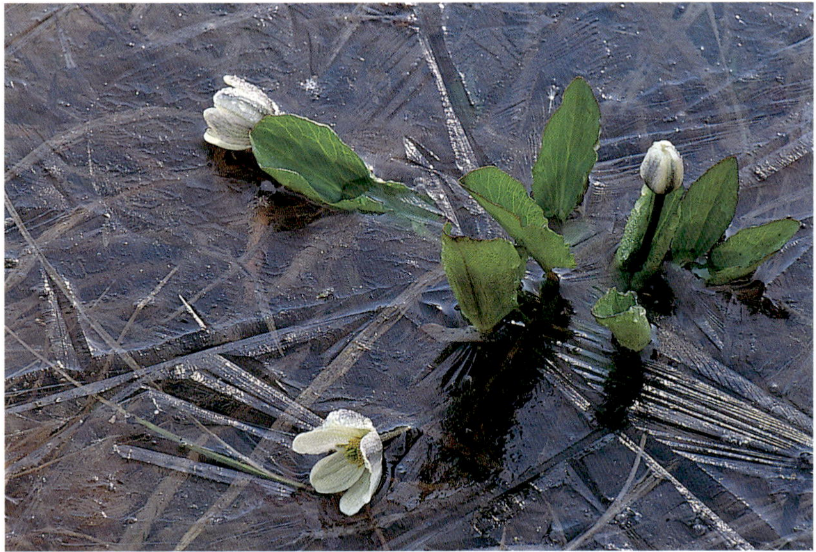

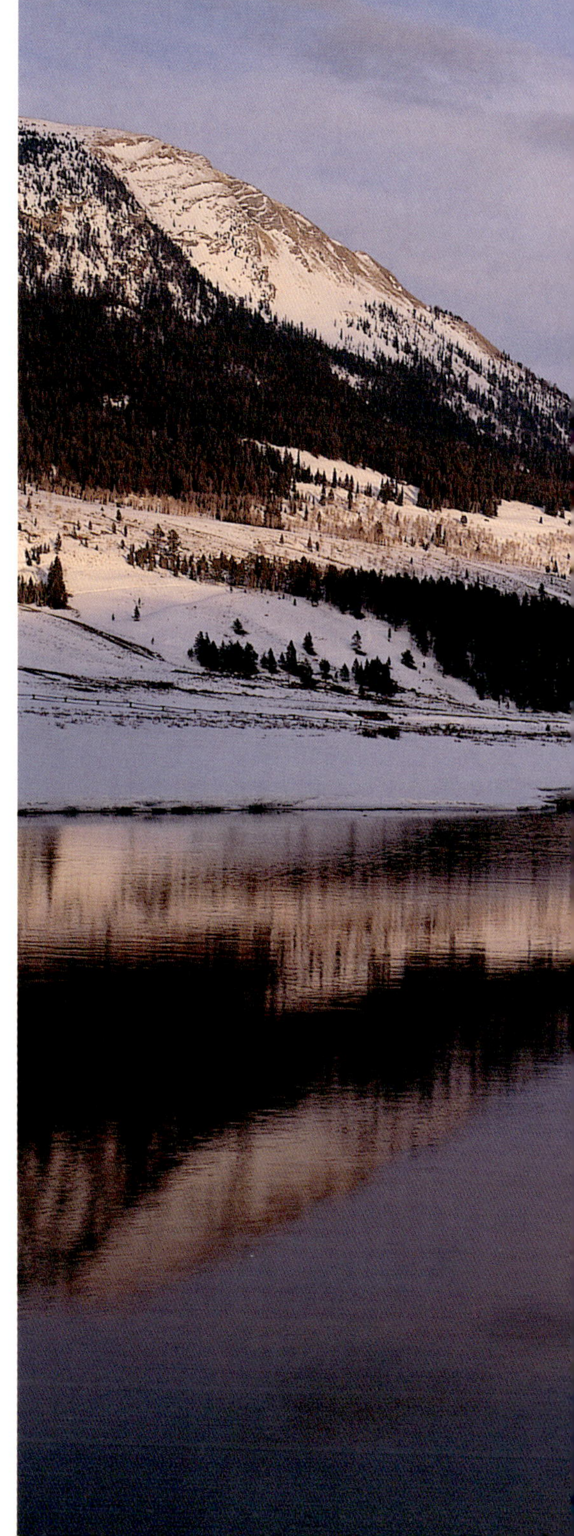

Above: Ice-encased marsh marigold, Hobbs Lake, Bridger Wilderness.
ELIZABETH BOEHM

Right: Winter on the Upper Green River.
FRED PFLUGHOFT

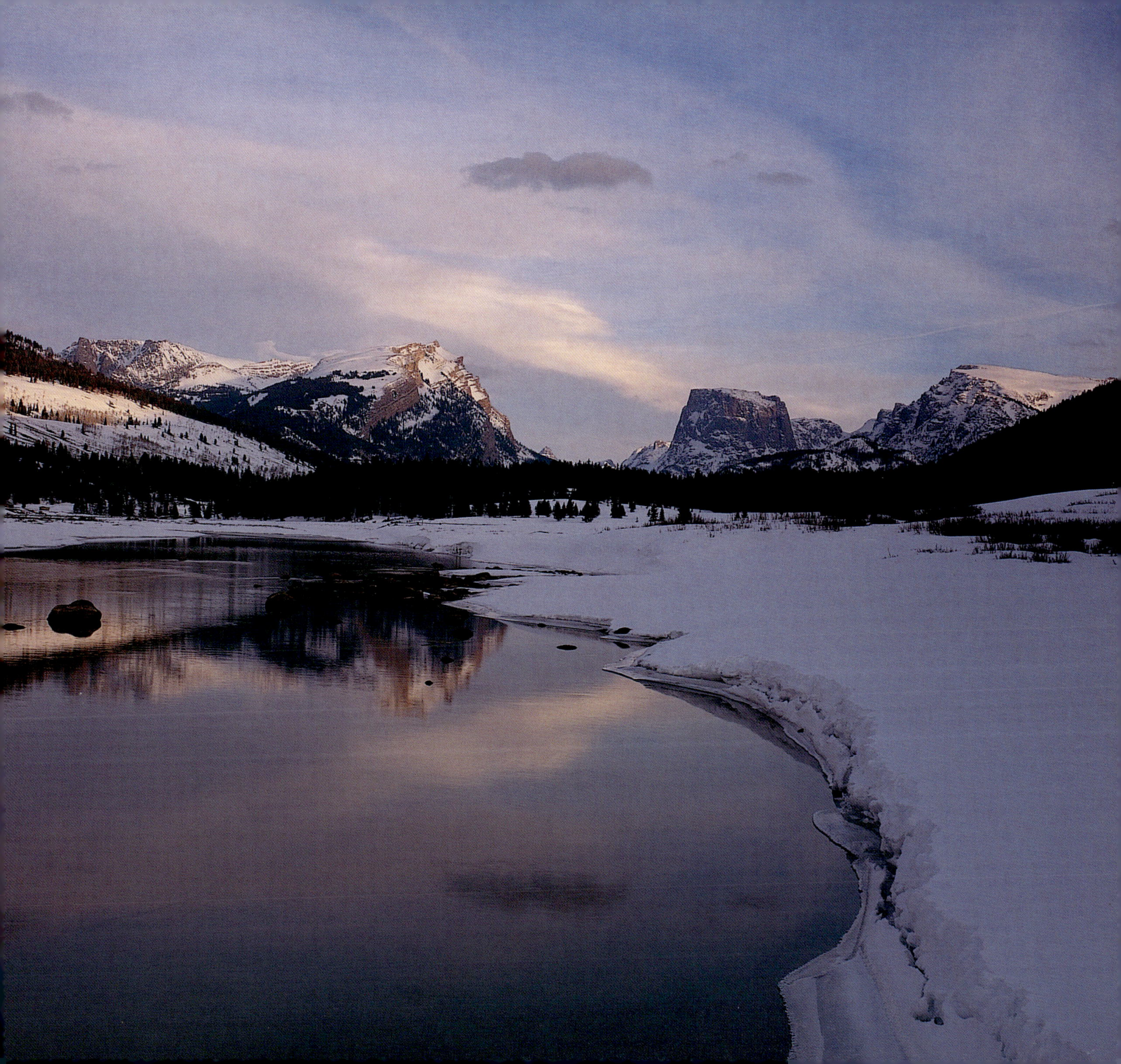

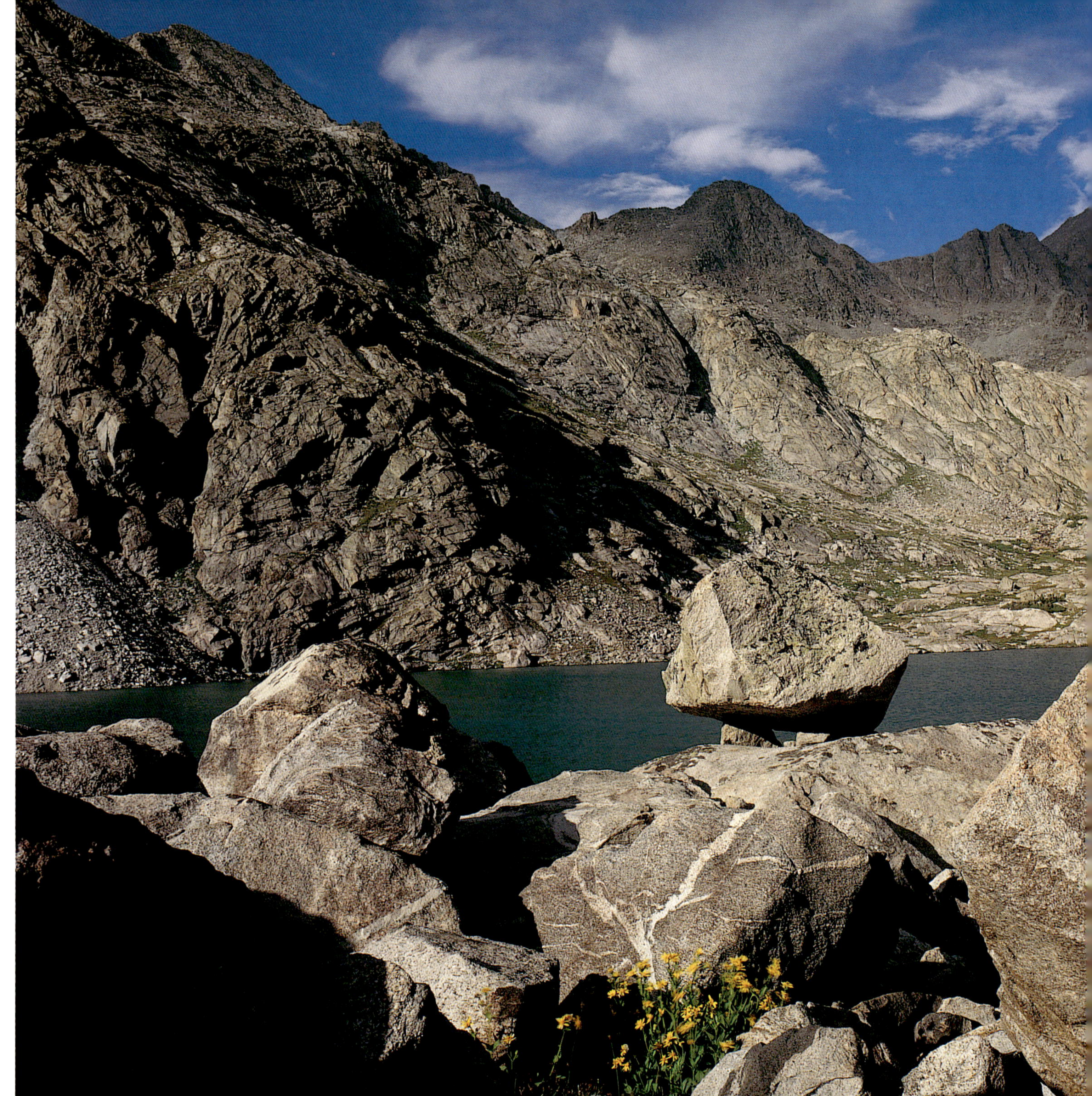

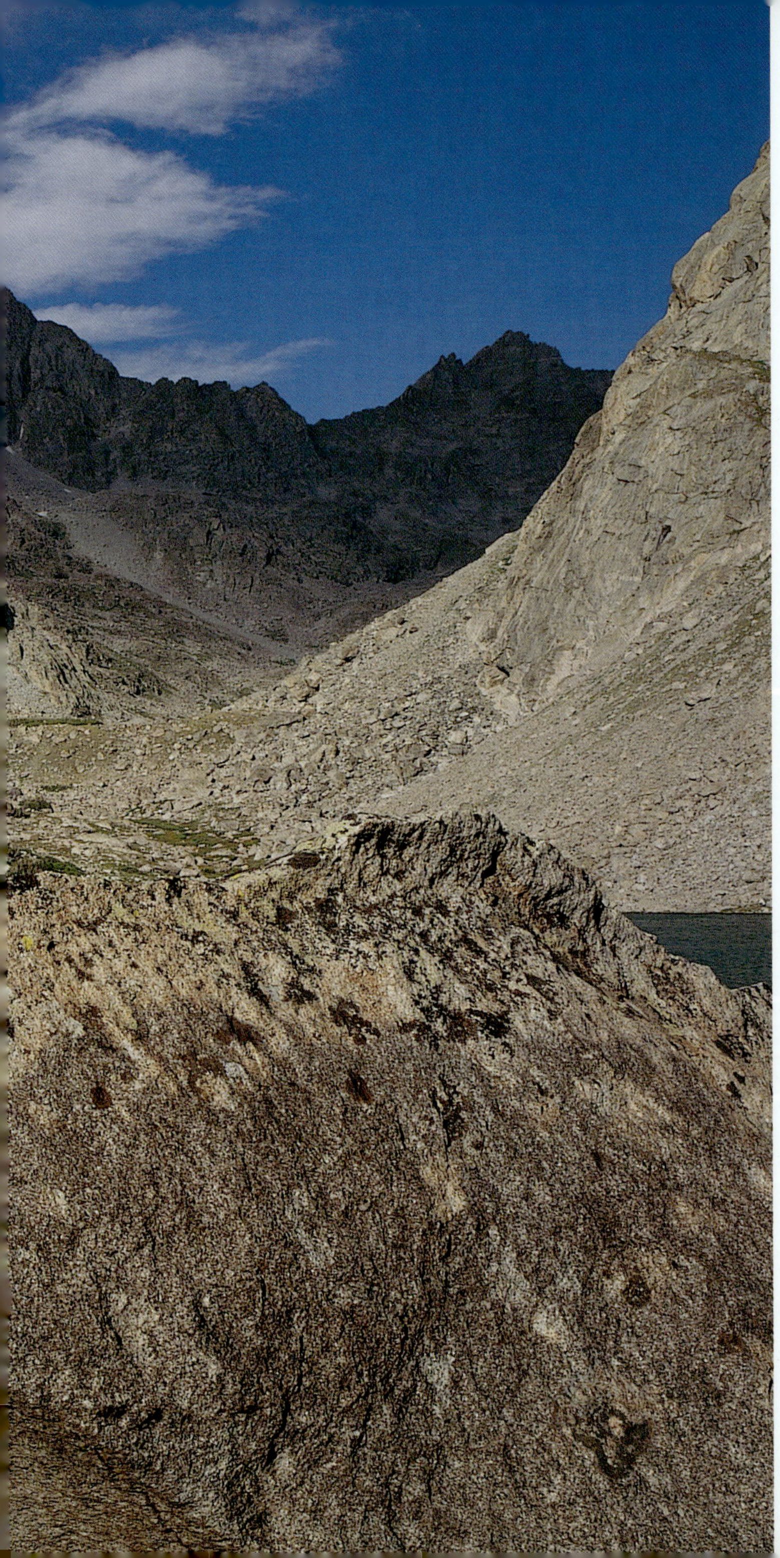

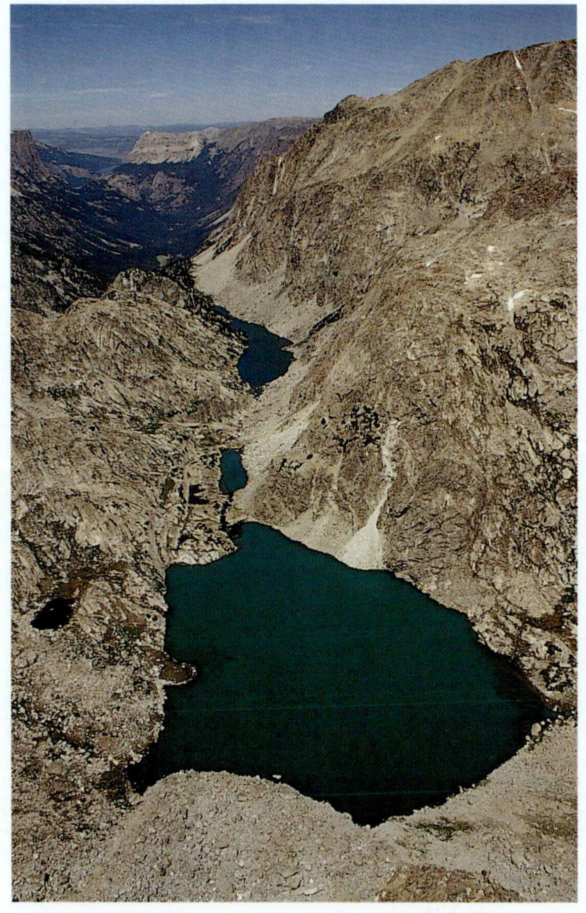

Above: Gazing down at Peak Lake from the summit of Stroud Peak. *FRED PFLUGHOFT*

Left: Split Mountain, 13,155 feet, rises above Peak Lake. *FRED PFLUGHOFT*

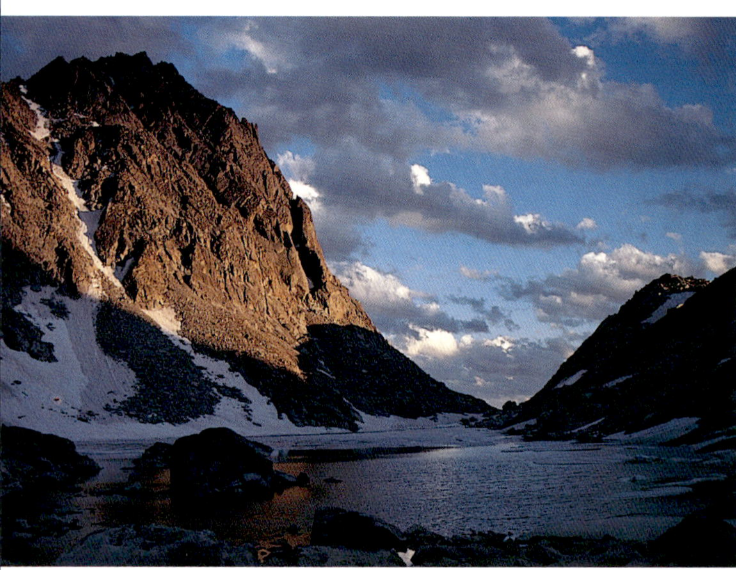

Above: An unnamed lake at the foot of G-17, bathed in the fading light of sunset.
FRED PFLUGHOFT

Right: The Green River reflects the image of stately Osborn Mountain.
FRED PFLUGHOFT

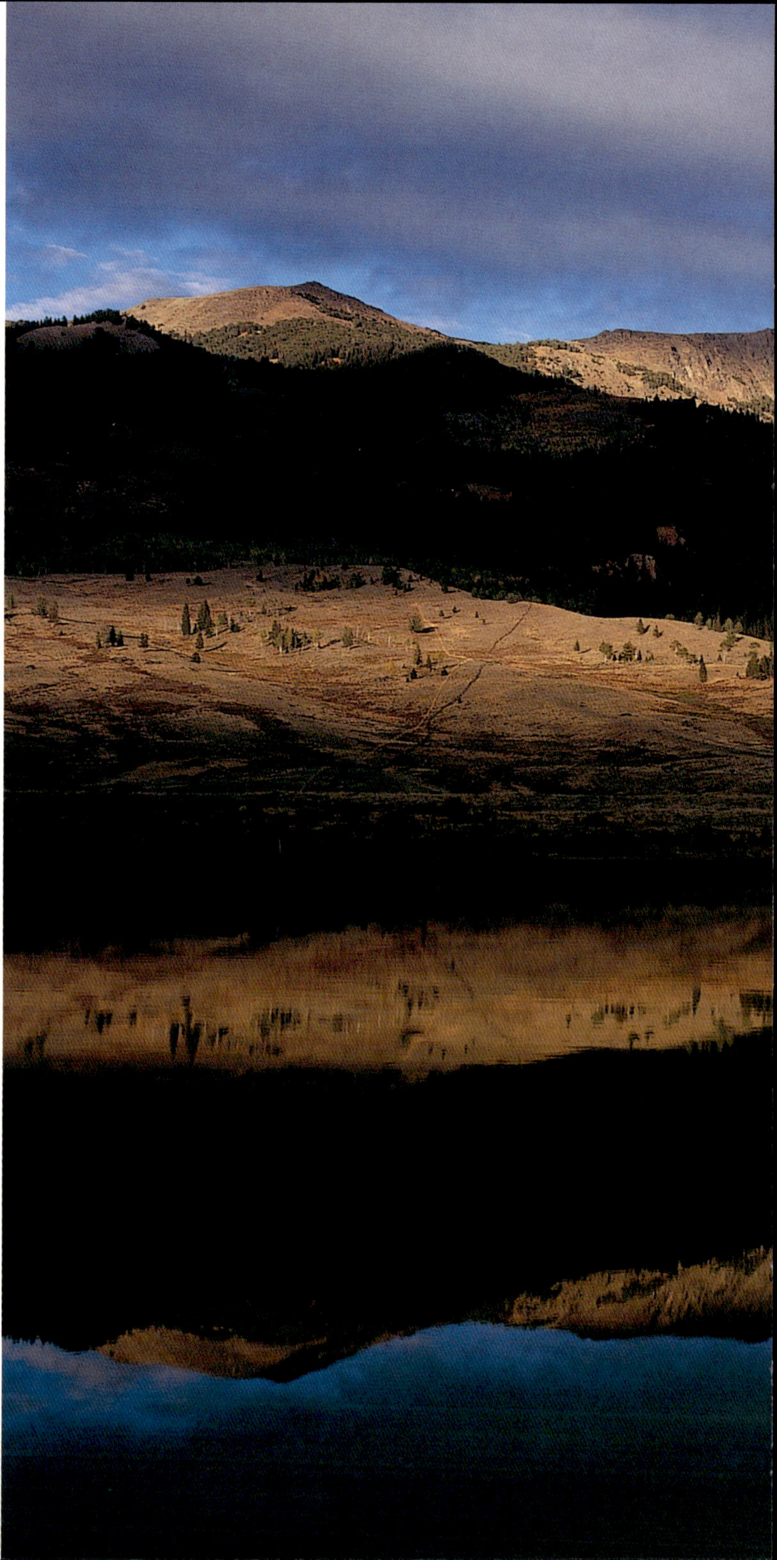

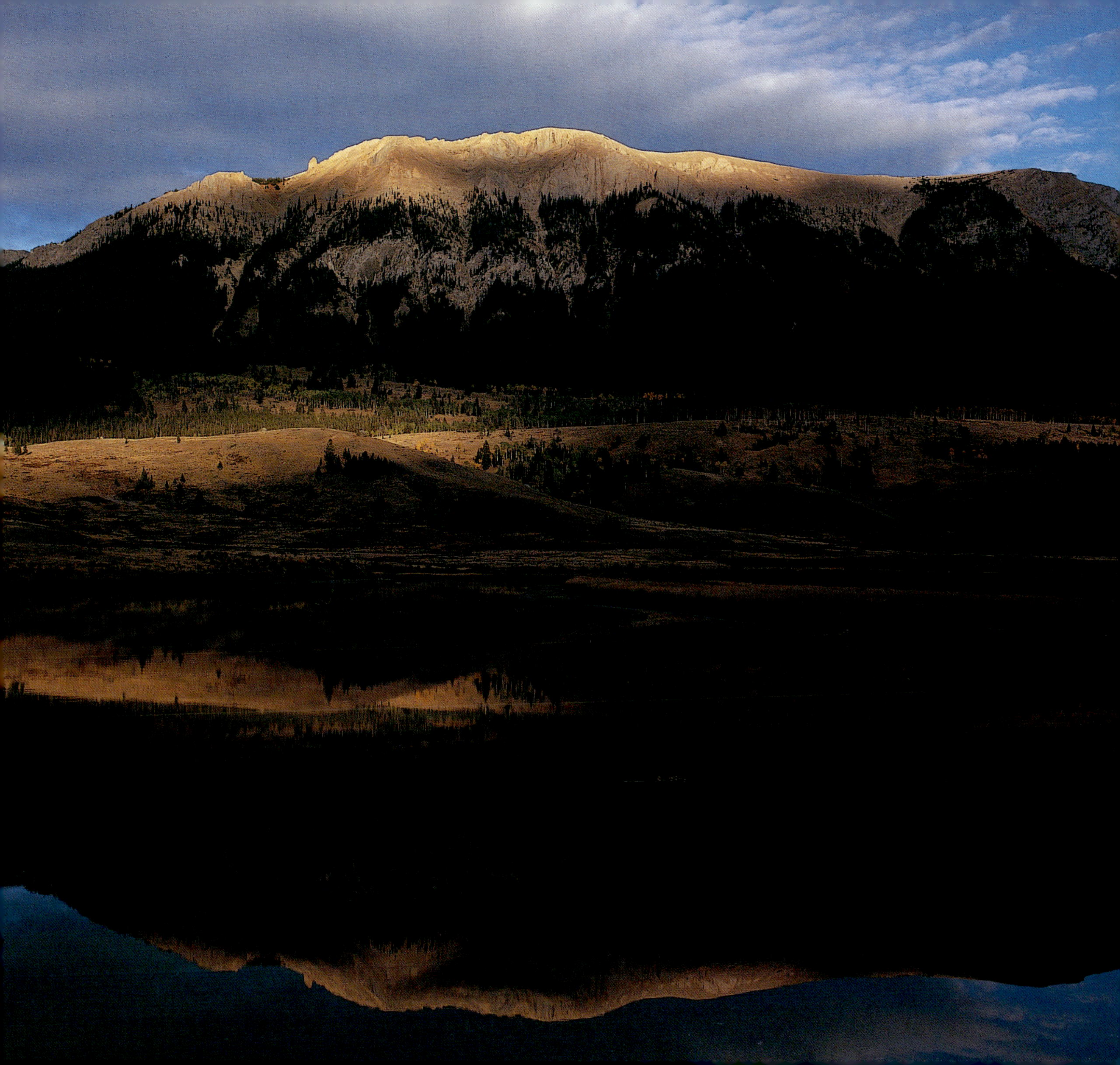

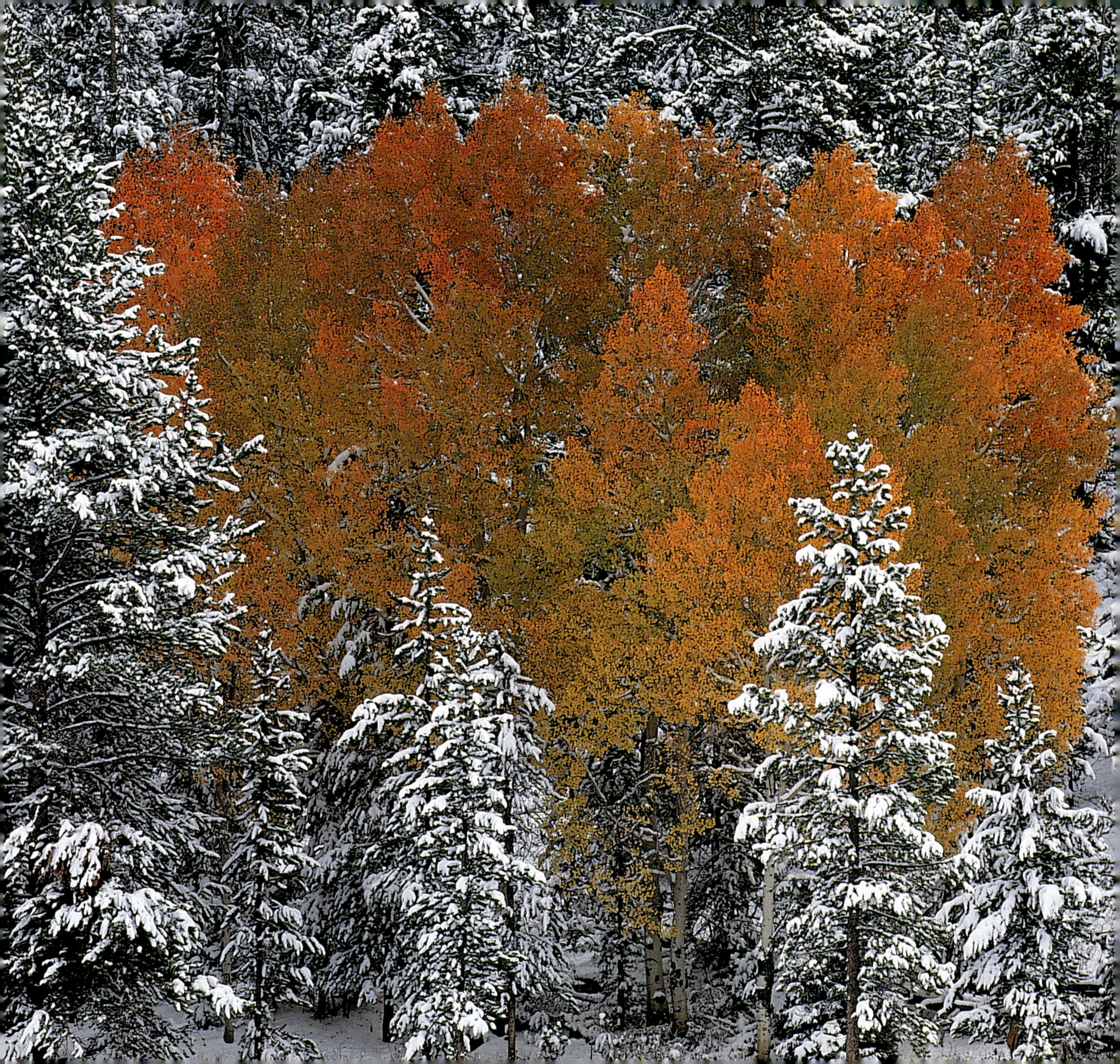

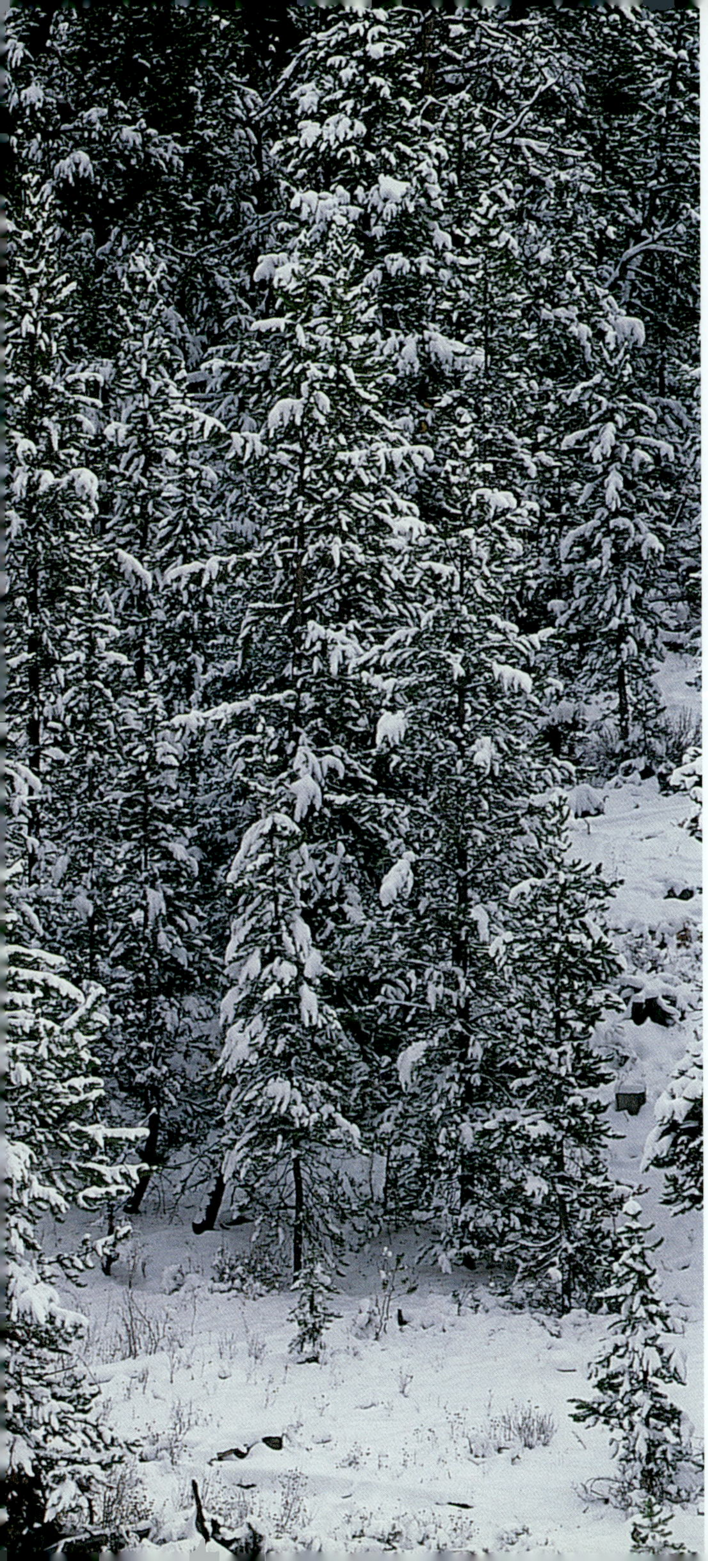

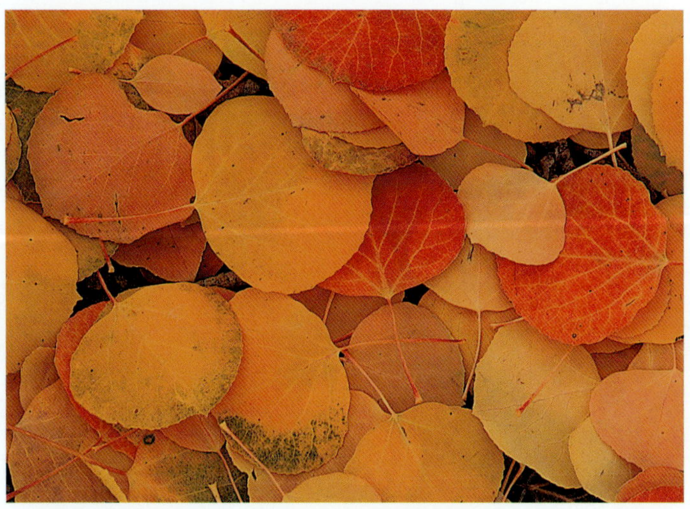

Above: Aspen leaves.
ELIZABETH BOEHM

Left: Winter comes early to the Upper Green River Valley, leaving these aspens a vibrant reminder of fall's glory.
ELIZABETH BOEHM

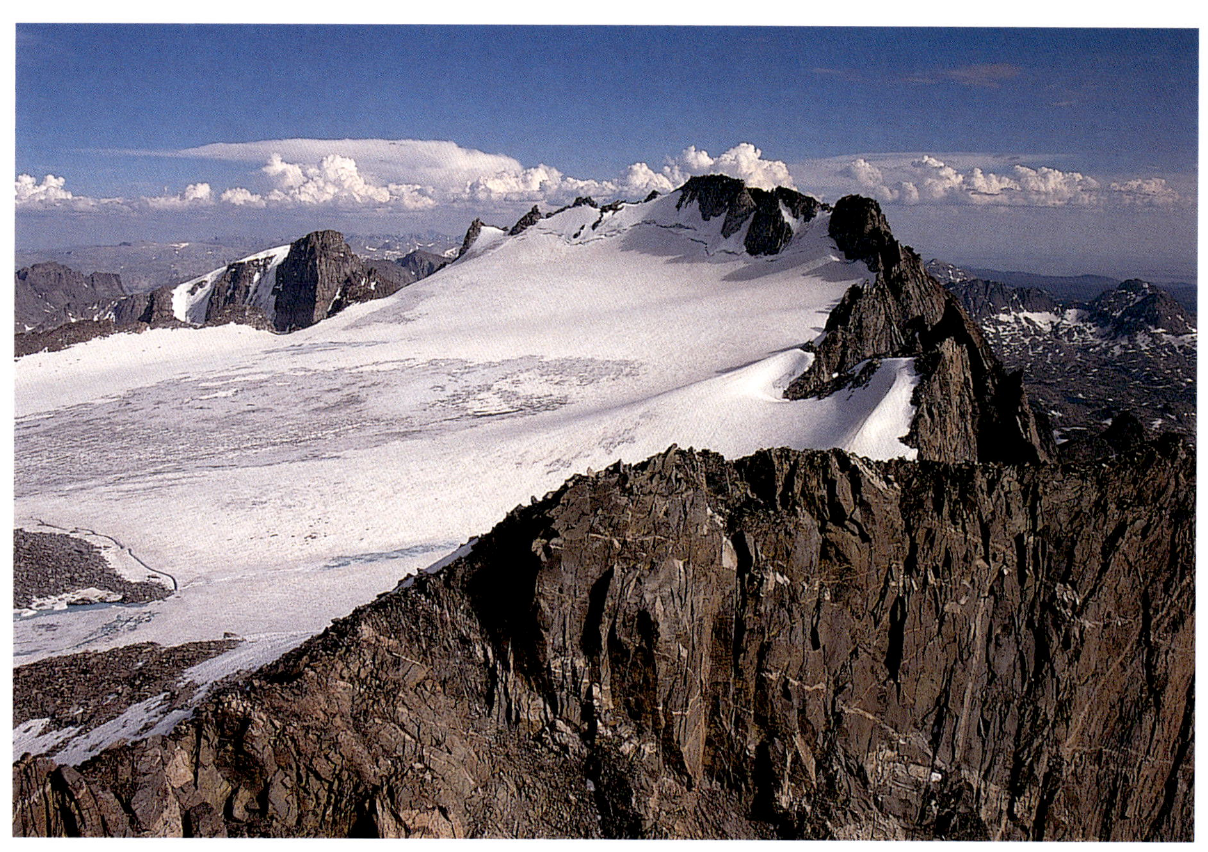

Above: The massive icefield of Upper Fremont Glacier spreads out below the jagged crest of Fremont Peak as viewed from the summit of Mount Sacagawea.
FRED PFLUGHOFT

Facing page: Rapid Lake nestled below Schiestler Peak.
FRED PFLUGHOFT

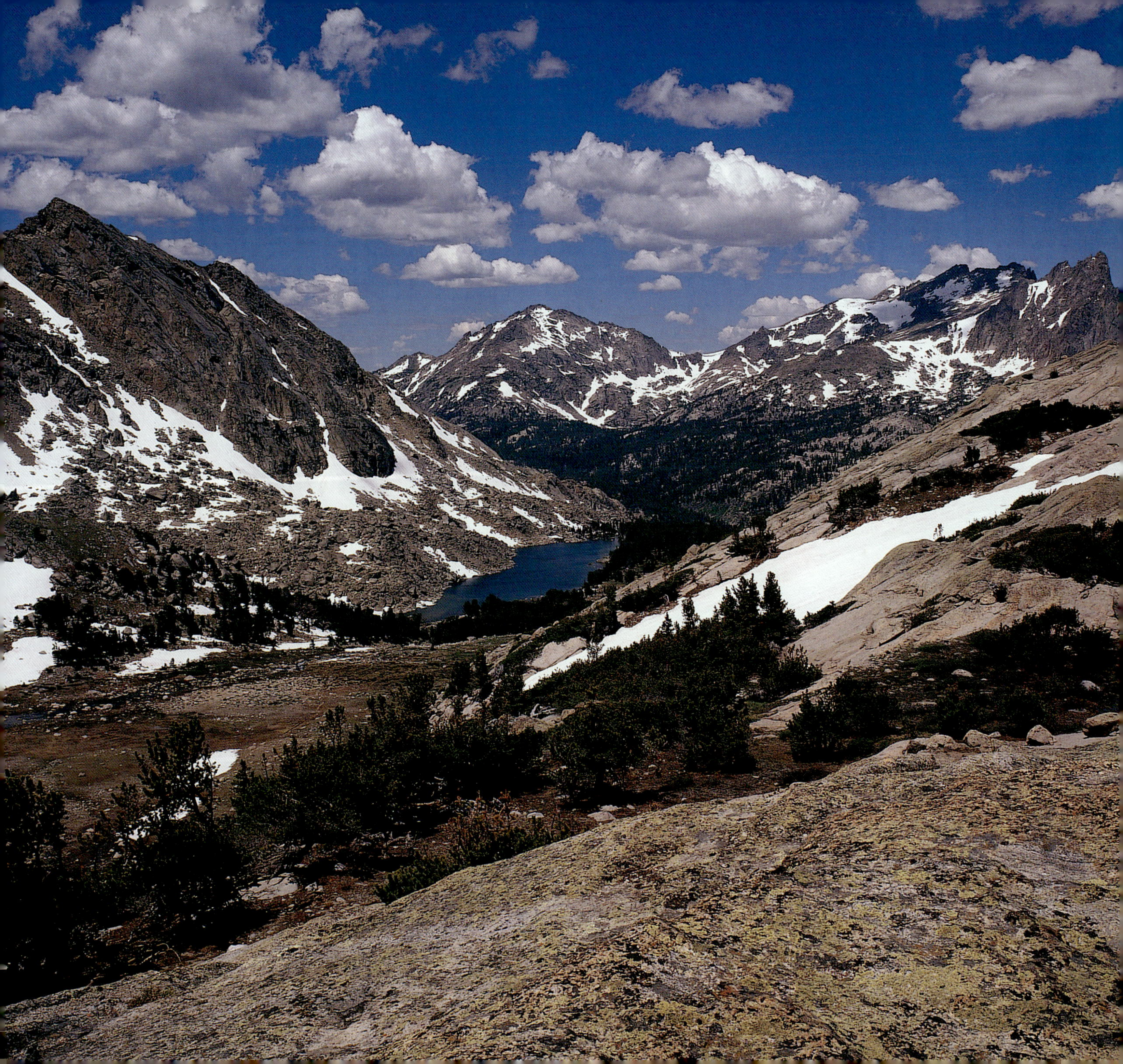

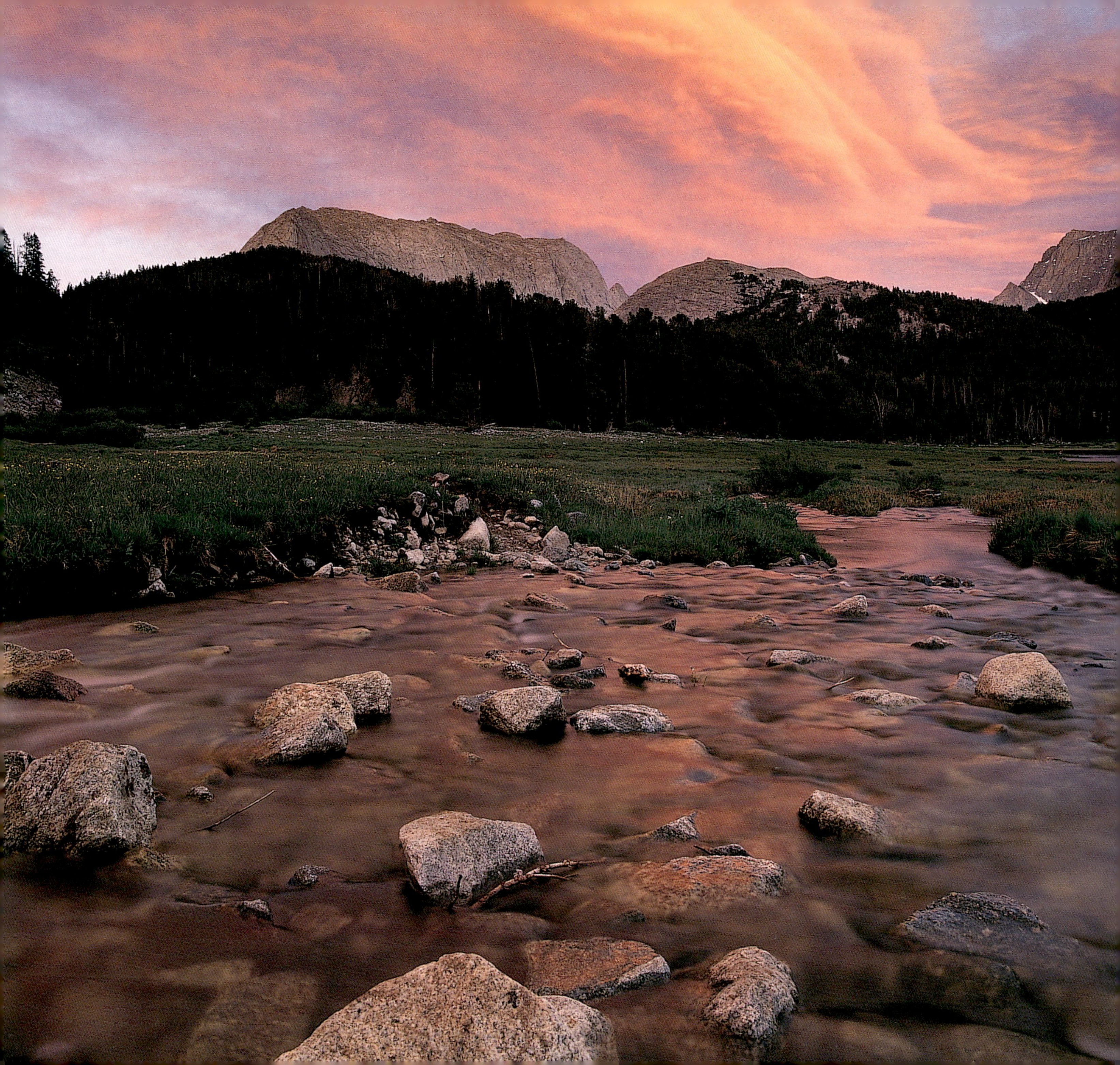

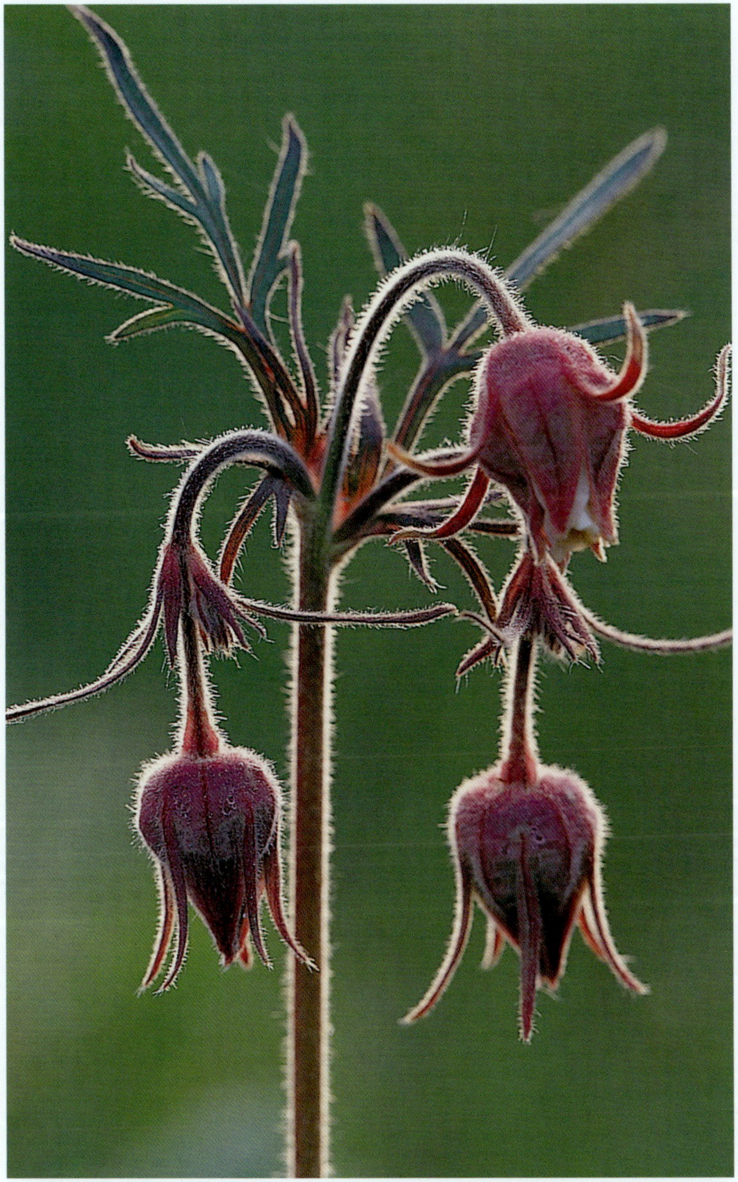

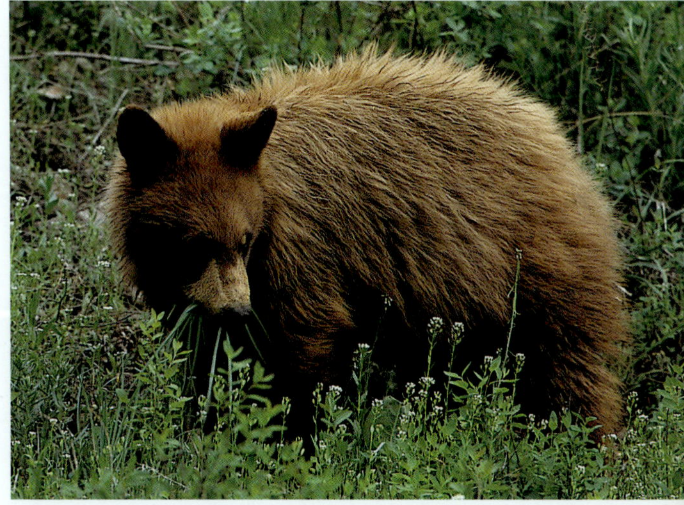

Above: Black bear cubs are born in winter dens in January or February, are weaned in August, and leave their mothers after the first year. *JOHN C. ERIKSSON*

Left: Prairie smoke, Upper Green River. The bell-like flowers turn upward, exposing whispy plumes that catch the wind and disperse seeds. *ELIZABETH BOEHM*

Facing page: A dramatic sunset near Big Sandy Lake, Bridger Wilderness. *DELSA SMITH ALLEN*

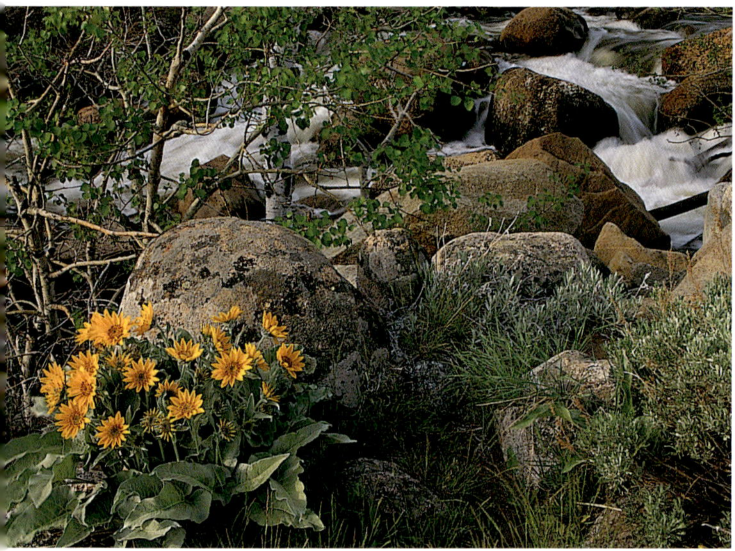

Above: Arrow-leaved balsamroot blooms beside the Popo Agie River, Sinks Canyon State Park.
FRED PFLUGHOFT

Right: The rugged shoreline of Fremont Lake. At 12 miles long, half a mile wide, and 600 feet deep, it is Wyoming's second-largest and one of the country's deepest lakes.
FRED PFLUGHOFT

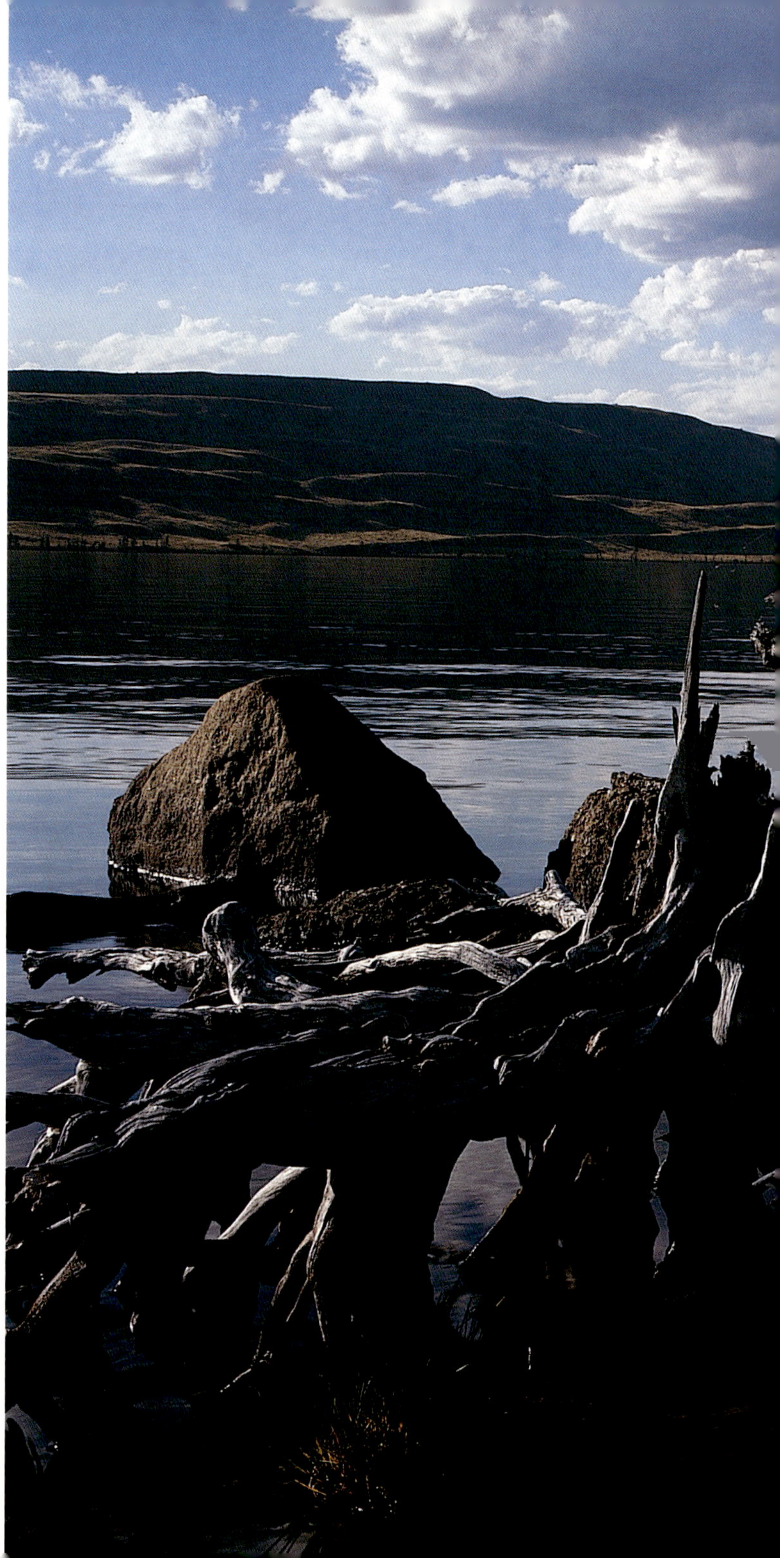

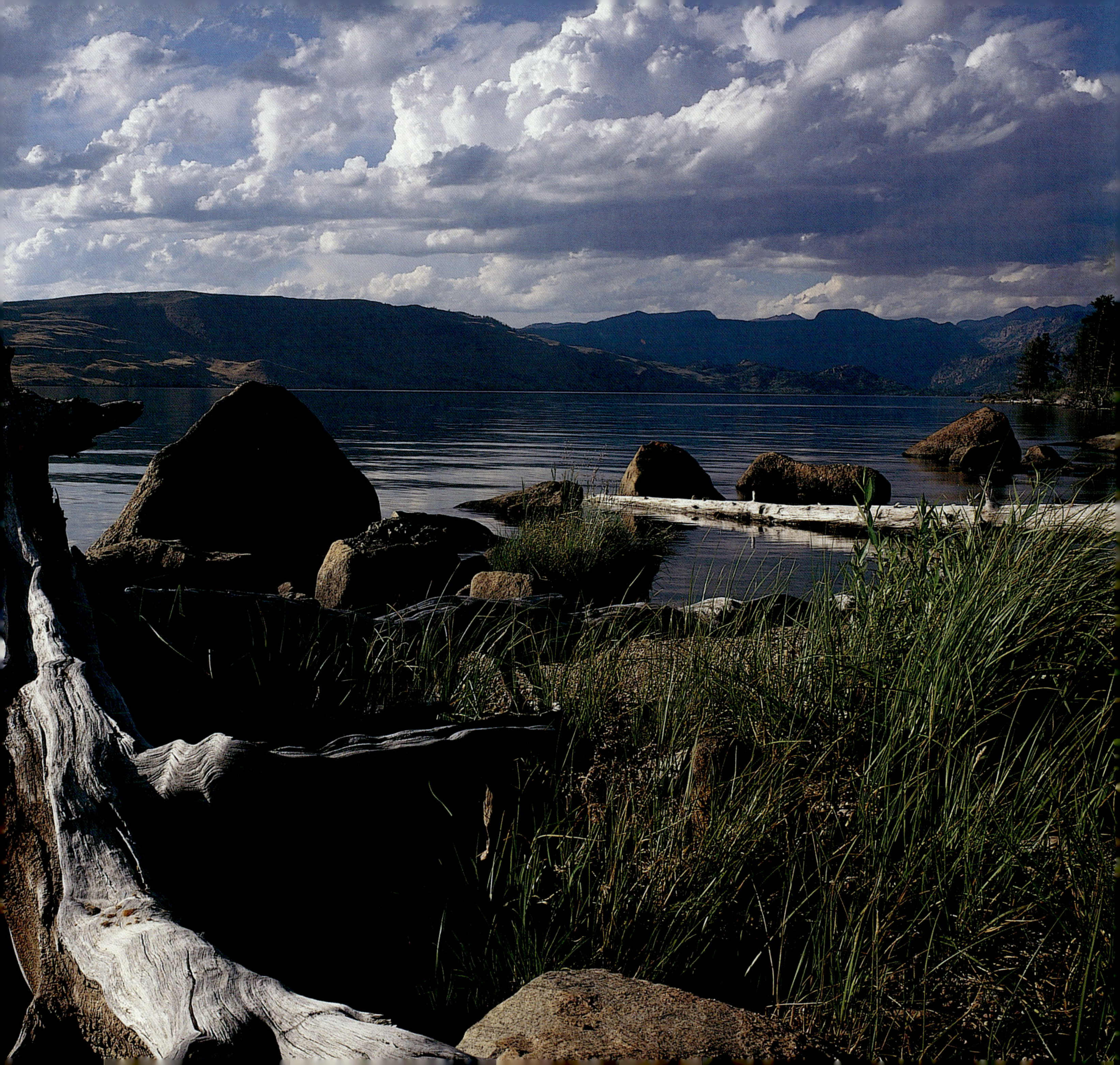

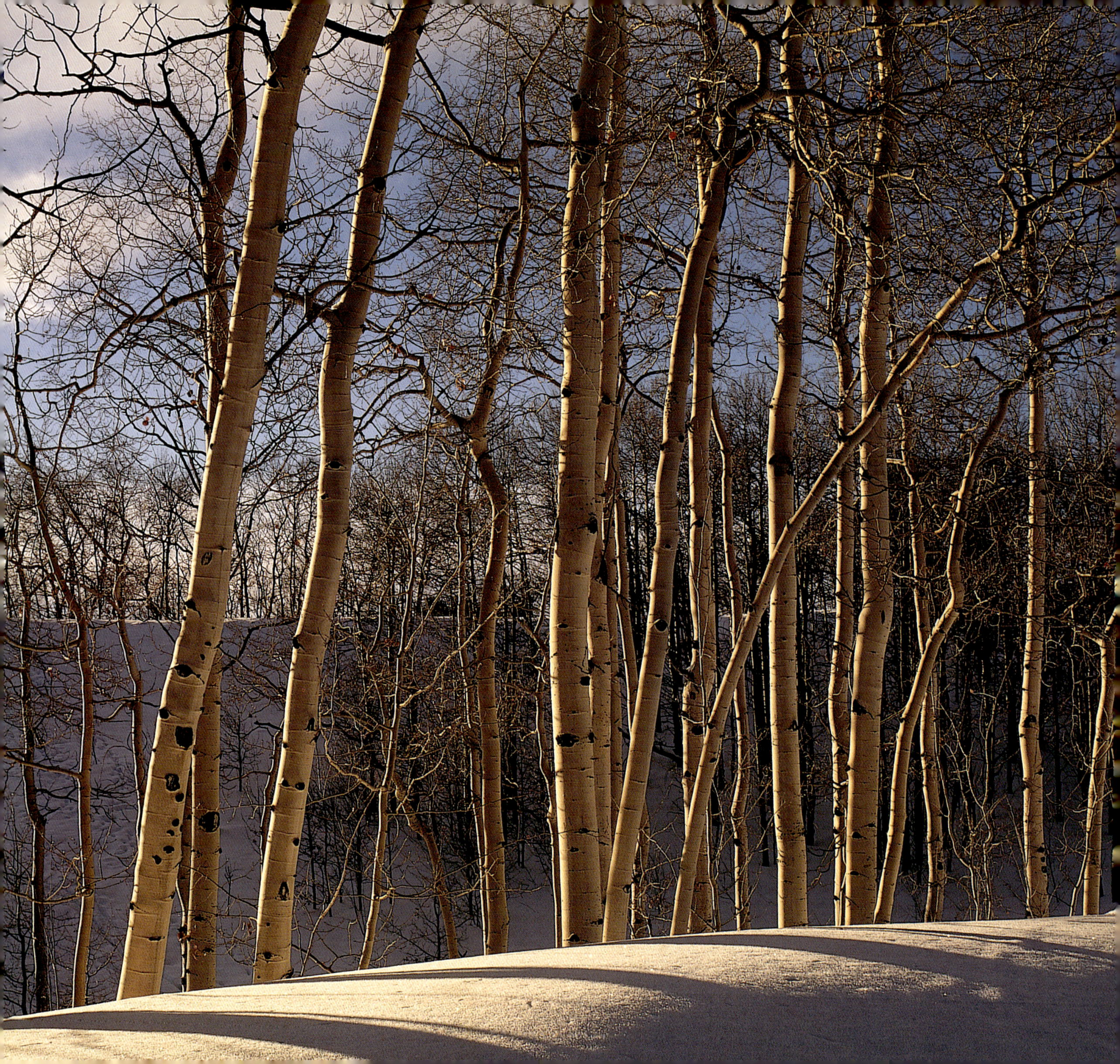

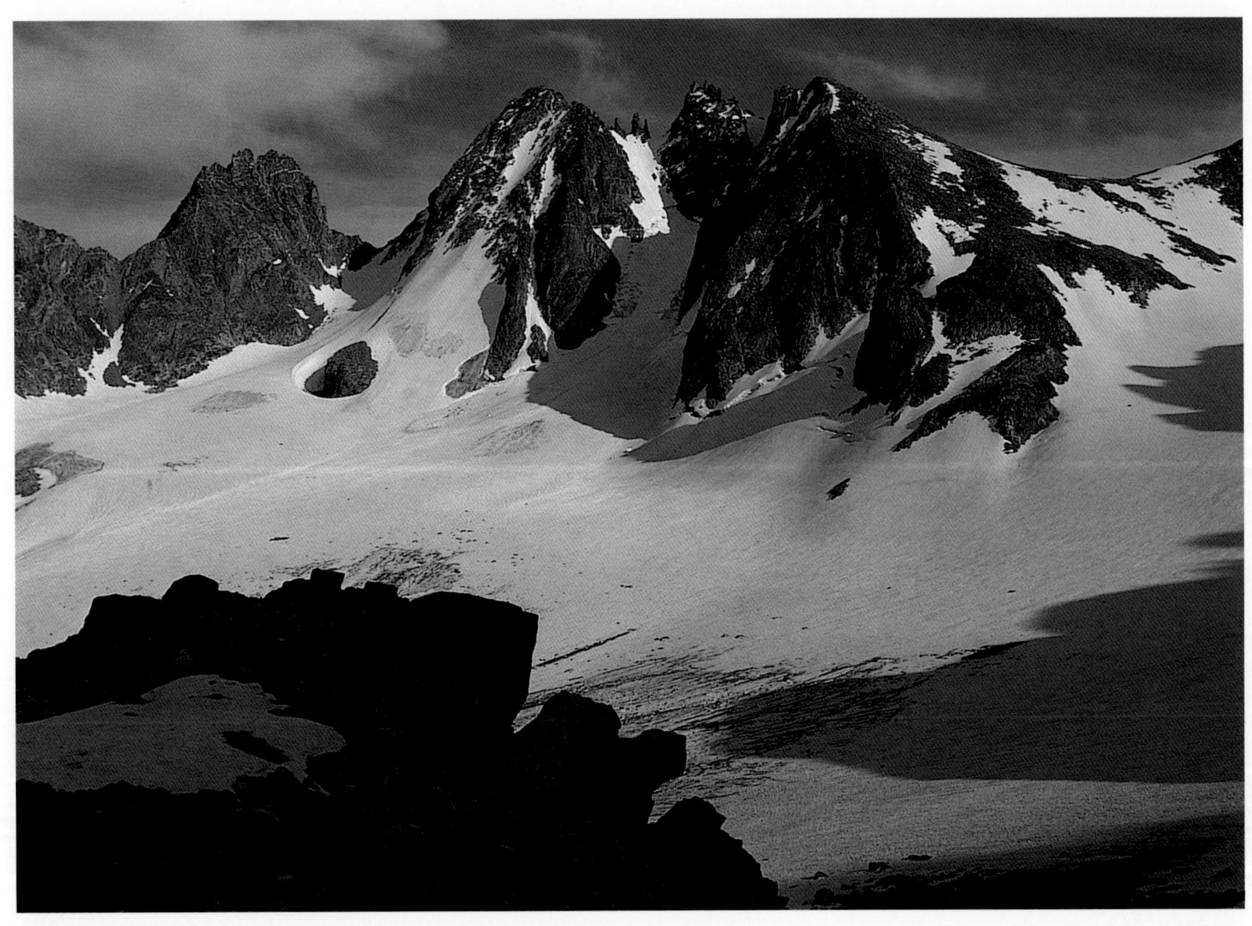

Above: Mt. Warren, Doublet, and Dinwoody peaks from Gooseneck Ridge. *FRED PFLUGHOFT*

Facing page: Aspens reach through a blanket of snow toward the winter sky, Bridger-Teton National Forest. *FRED PFLUGHOFT*

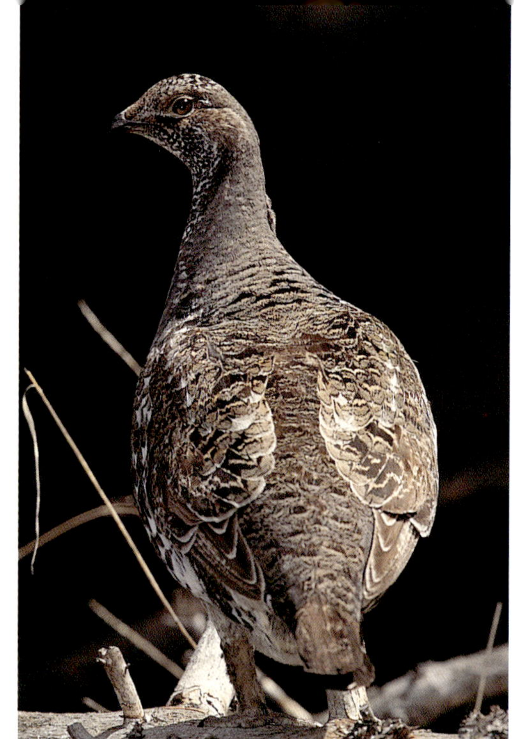

Right: Blue grouse wanders the Wind River woodlands.
JOHN C. ERIKSSON

Below: Glover Peak, Wind River Mountains.
FRED PFLUGHOFT

Facing page: Pronghorn Peak reflected in Lee Lake.
BEN FRANKLIN

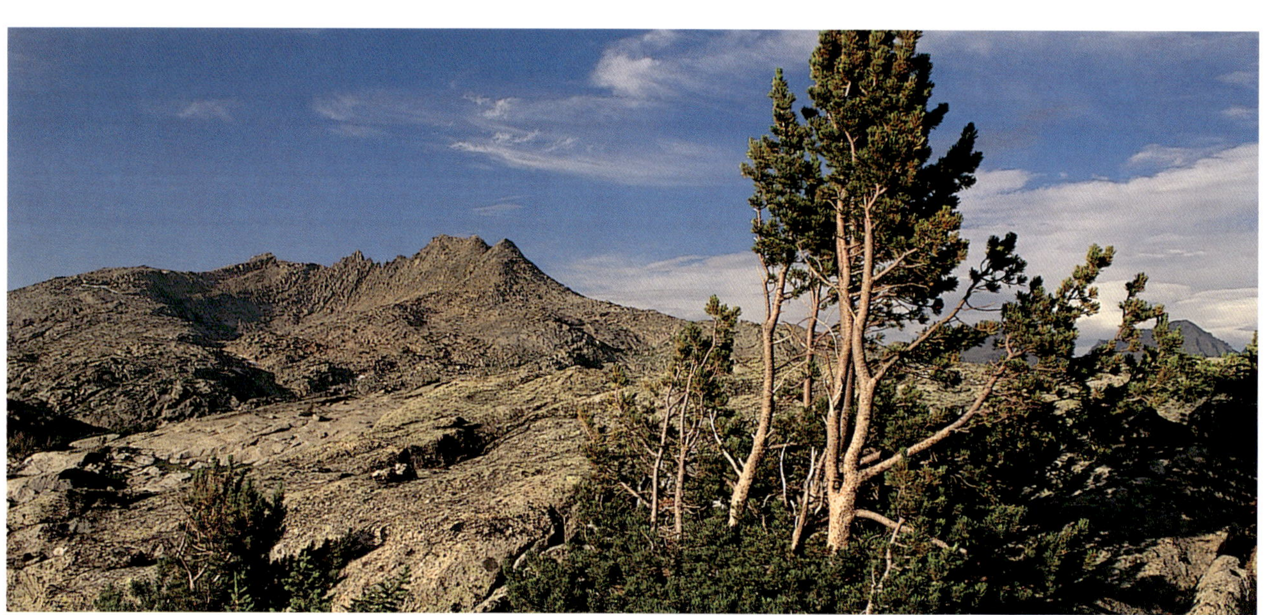

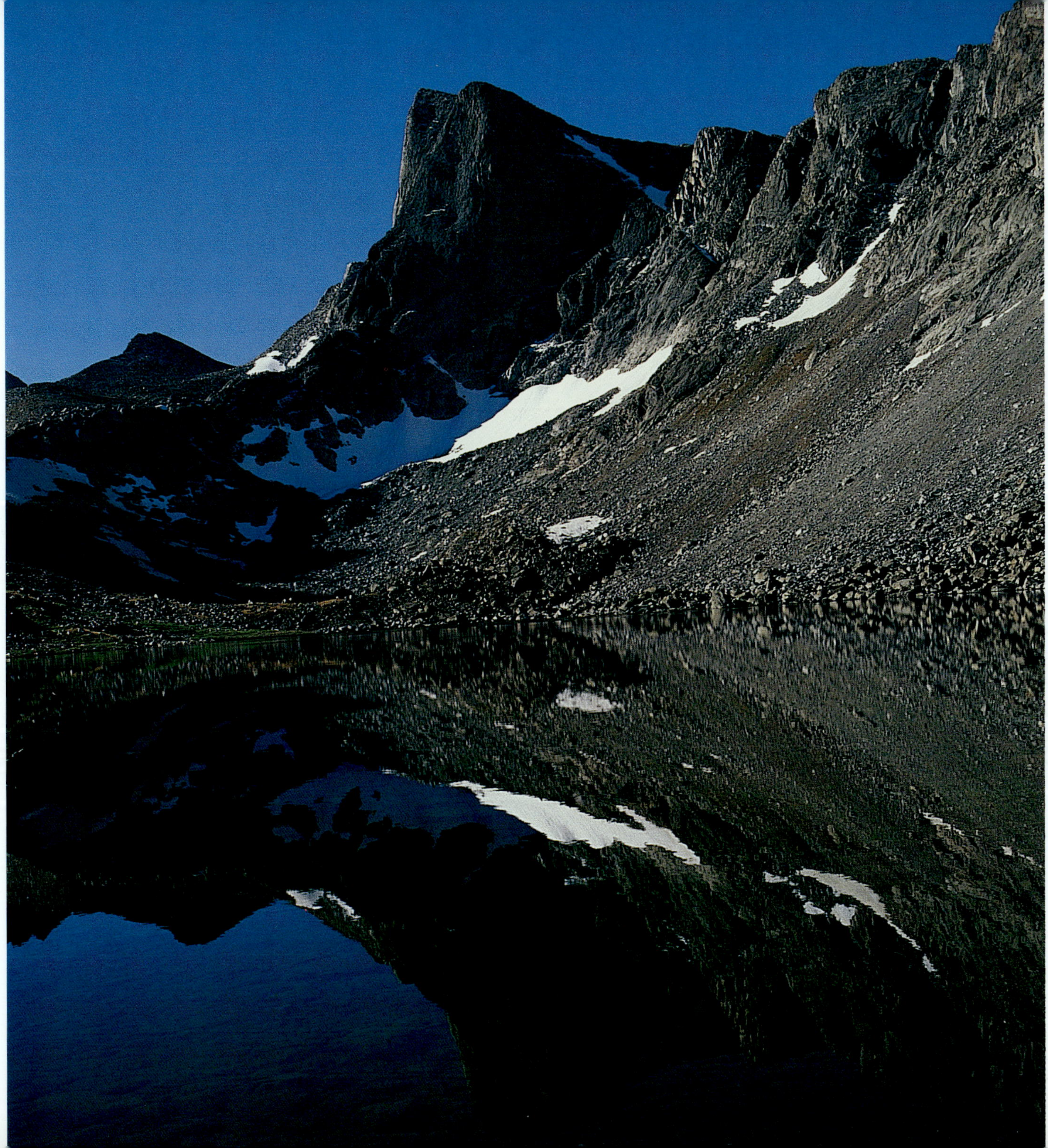

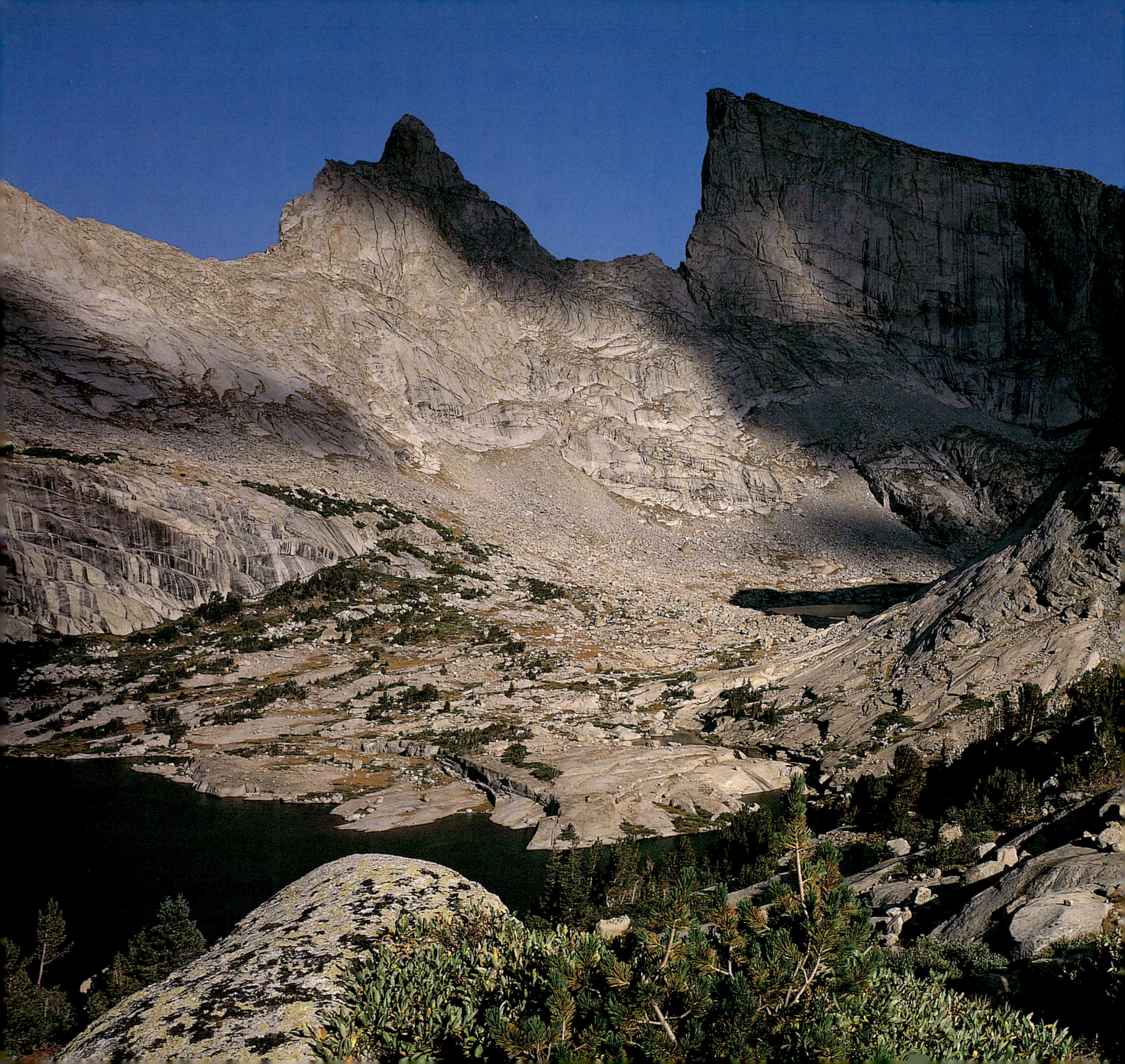

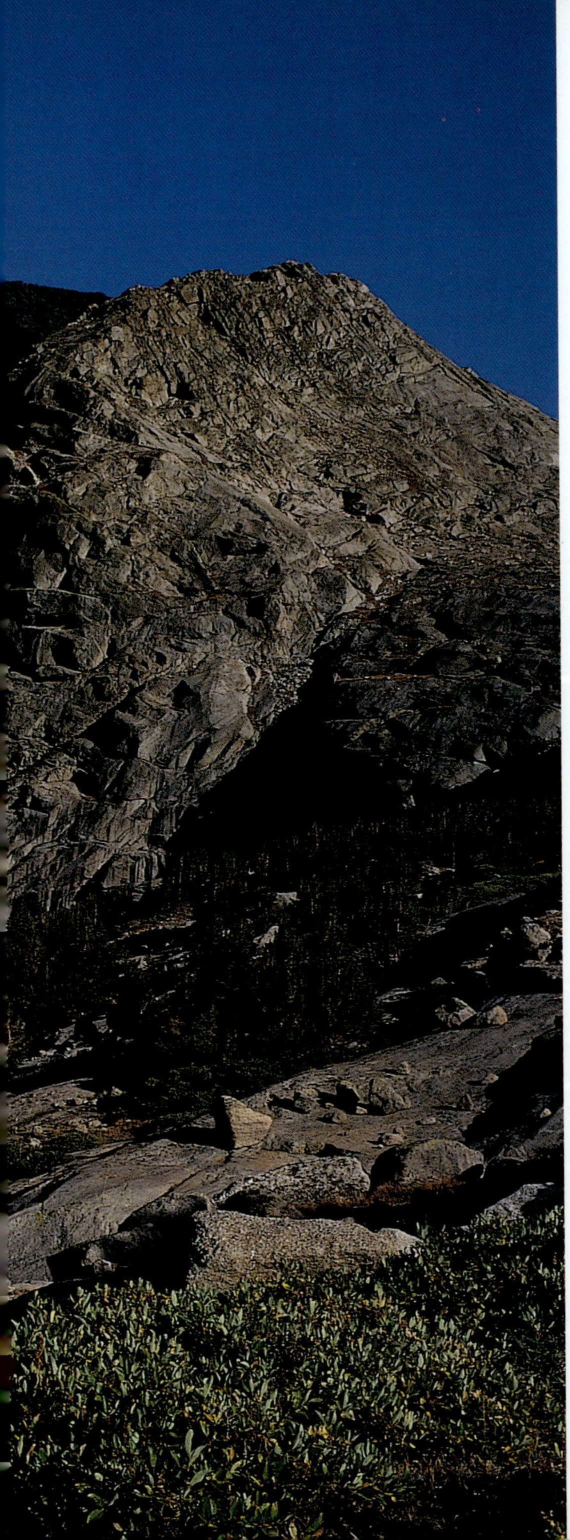

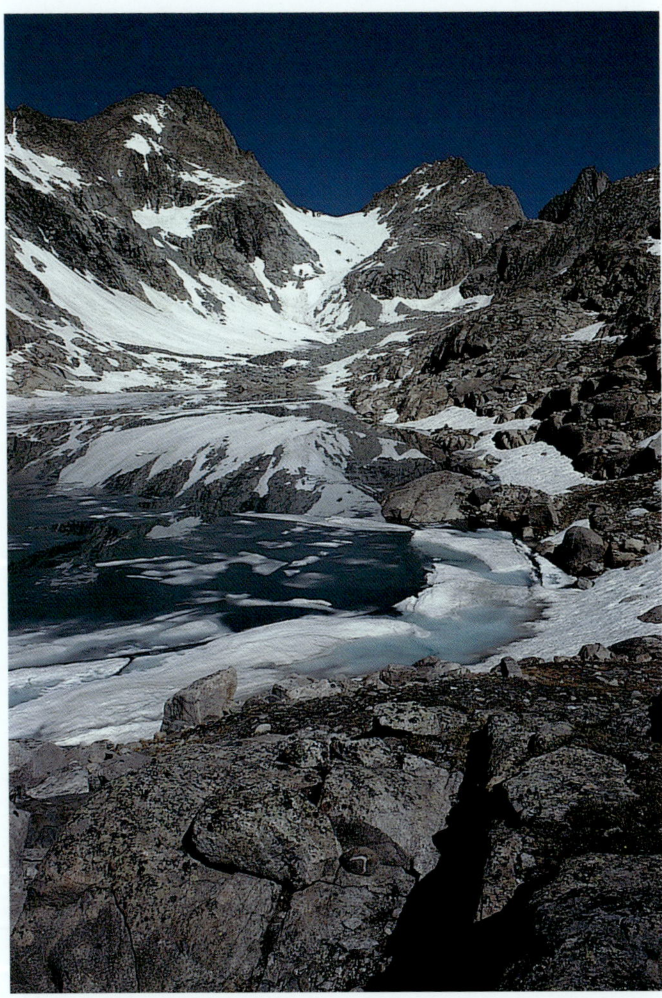

Above: American Legion and Winifred peaks overlook Summer Ice Lake. American Legion Peak is also known as Buchtel, named after Henry Buchtel, who made the first ascent in 1930.
FRED PFLUGHOFT

Left: Steeple and East Temple peaks above Deep Lake, Bridger Wilderness. *FRED PFLUGHOFT*

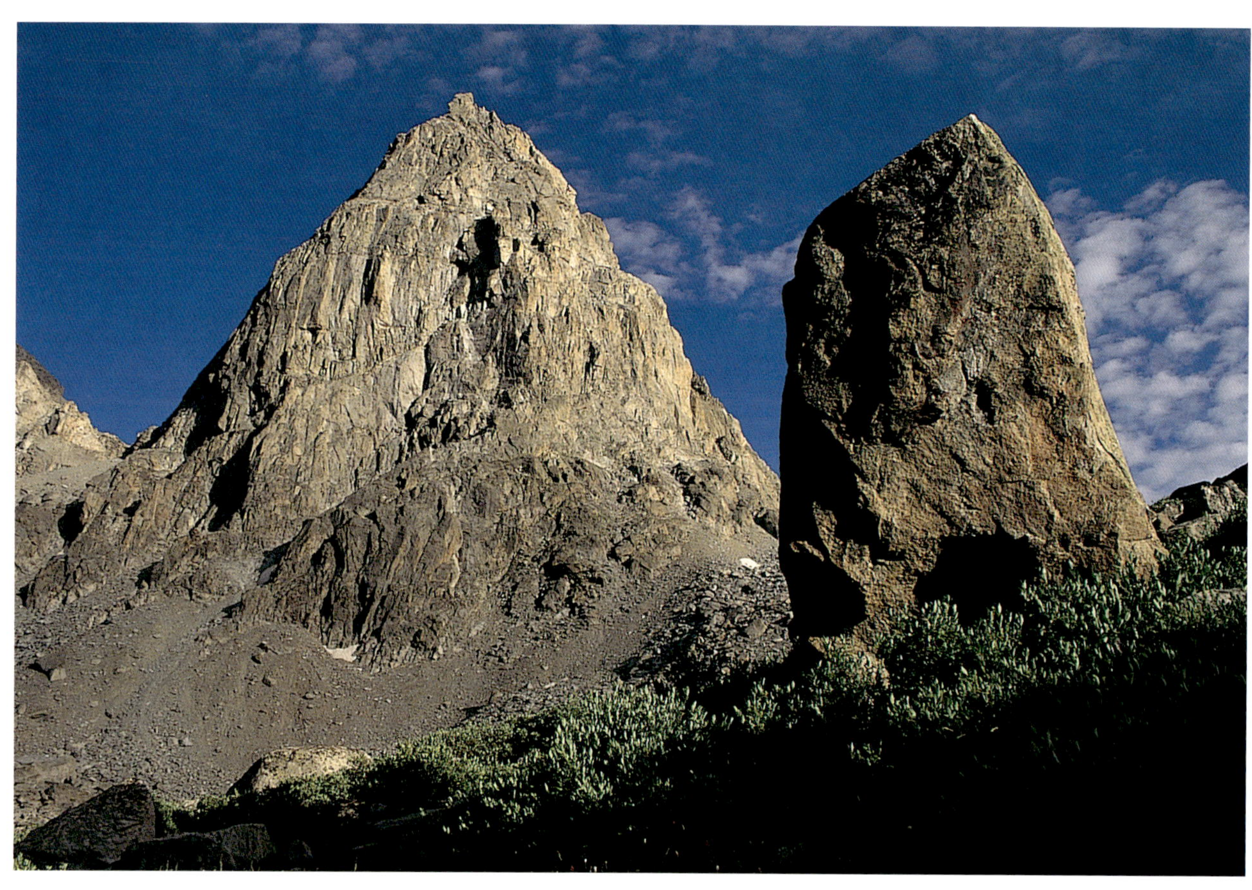

Above: Glacial erratic mirrors the profile of Stroud Peak.
FRED PFLUGHOFT

Facing page: Warbonnet Peak and Warrior I and II rise precipitously to form Cirque of the Towers, an imposing challenge for climbers, Popo Agie Wilderness.
FRED PFLUGHOFT

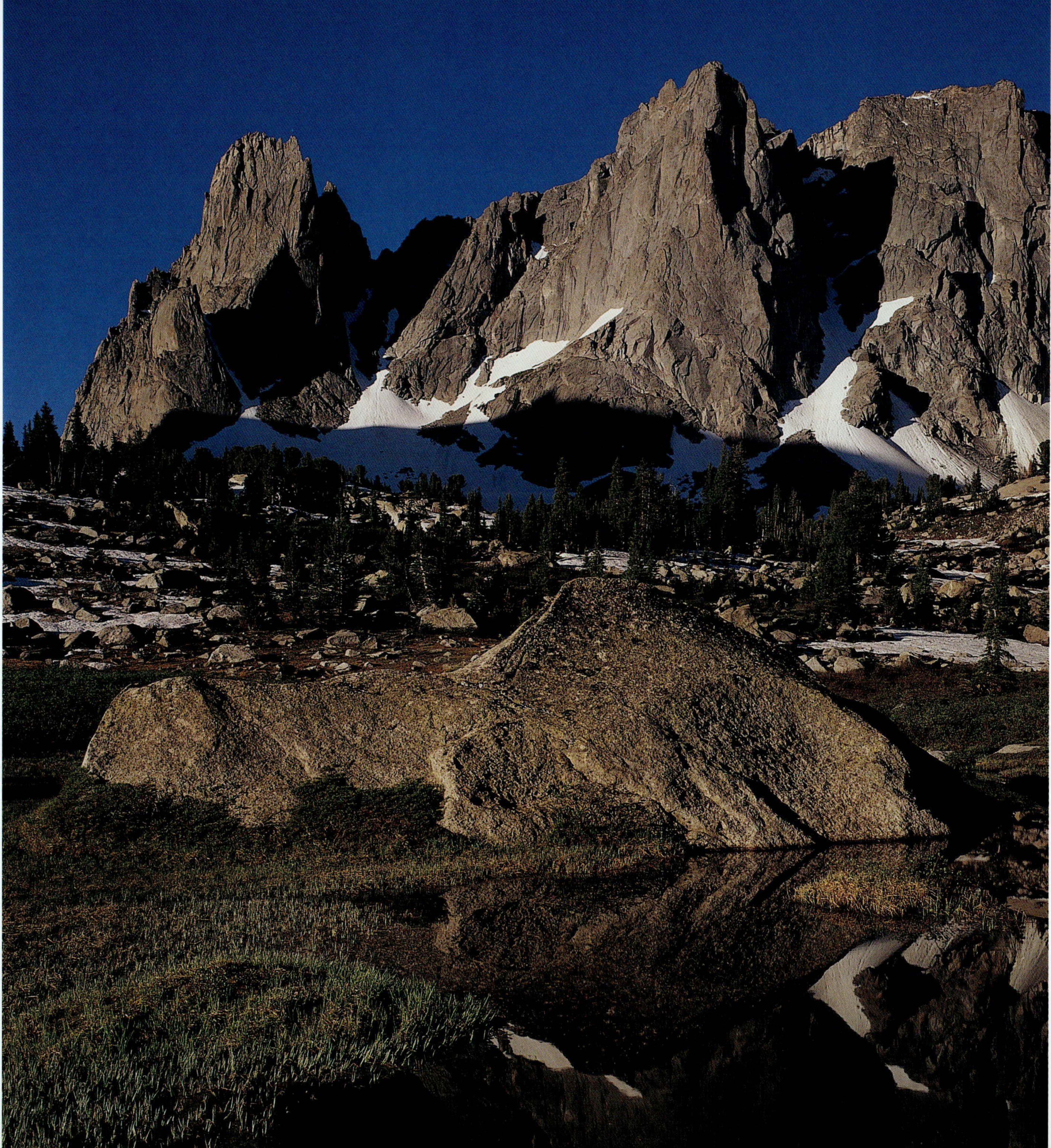

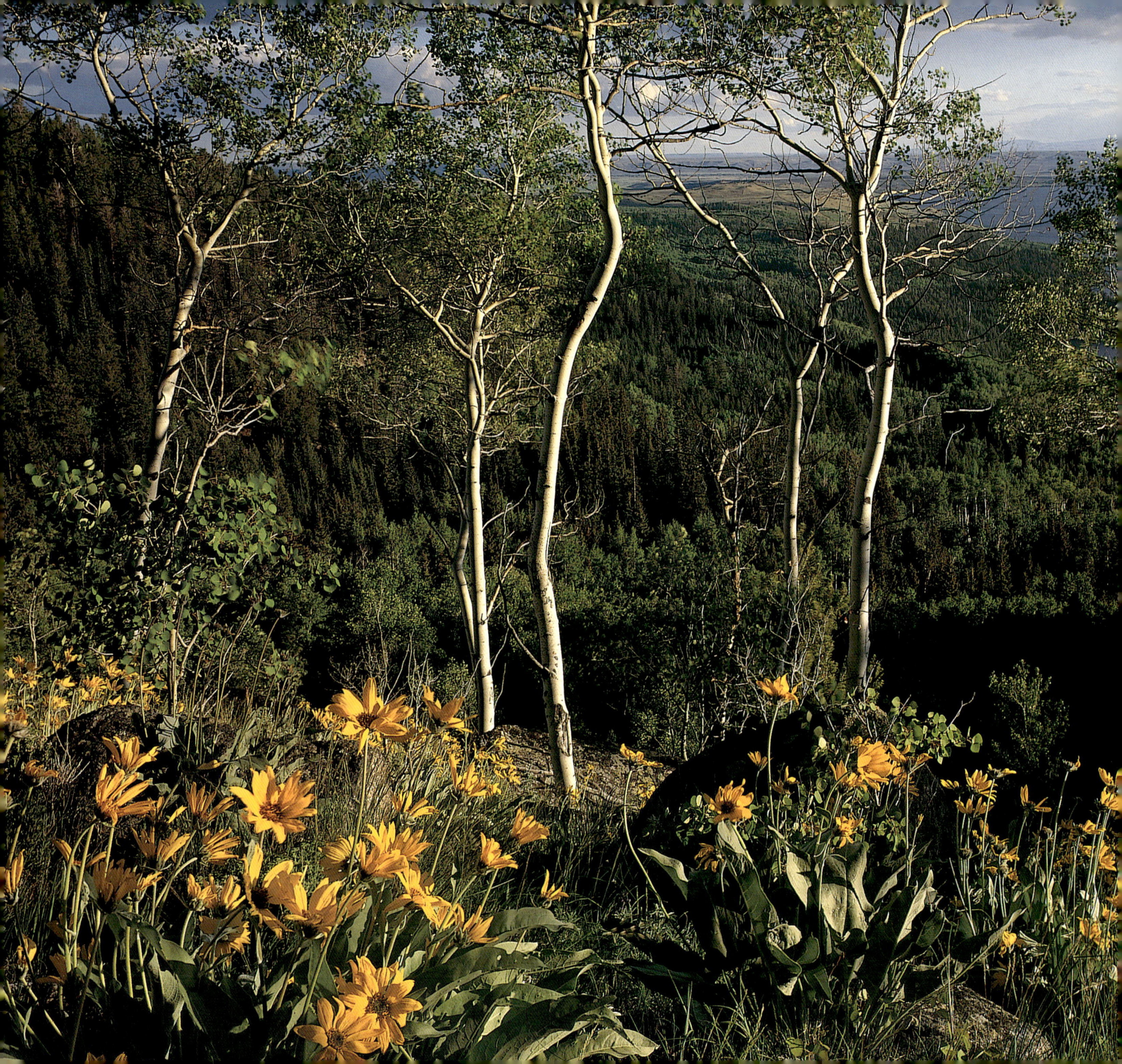

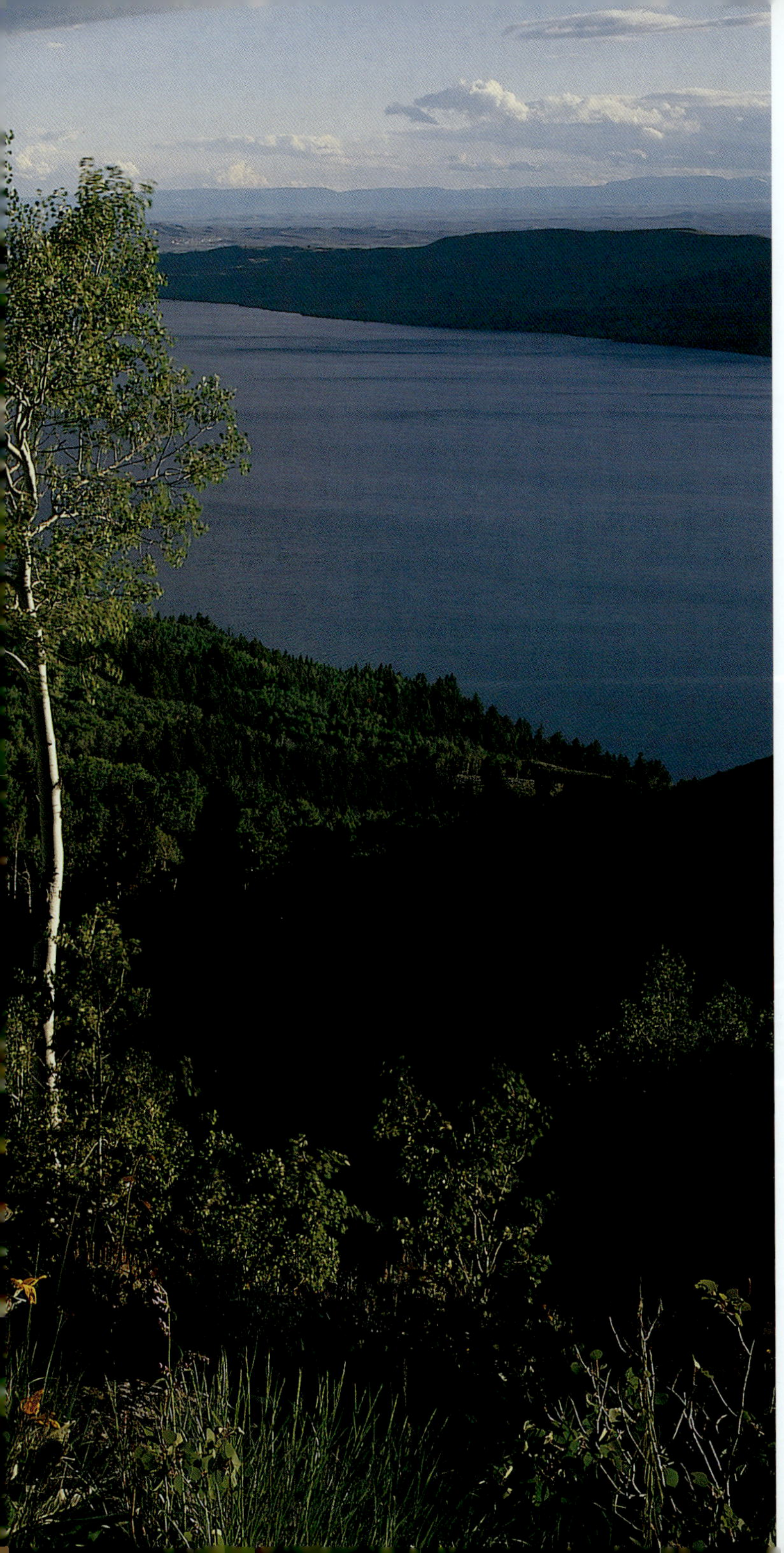

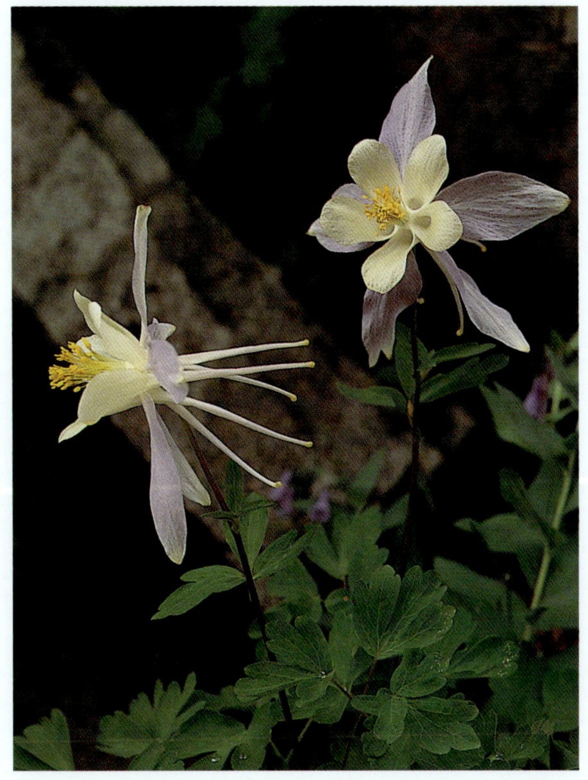

Above: The showy blossoms of the columbine.
FRED PFLUGHOFT

Left: Arrow-leaved balsamroot above Fremont Lake. The lake is named after John C. Fremont, who surveyed the area in 1842 while mapping the Oregon Trail.
FRED PFLUGHOFT

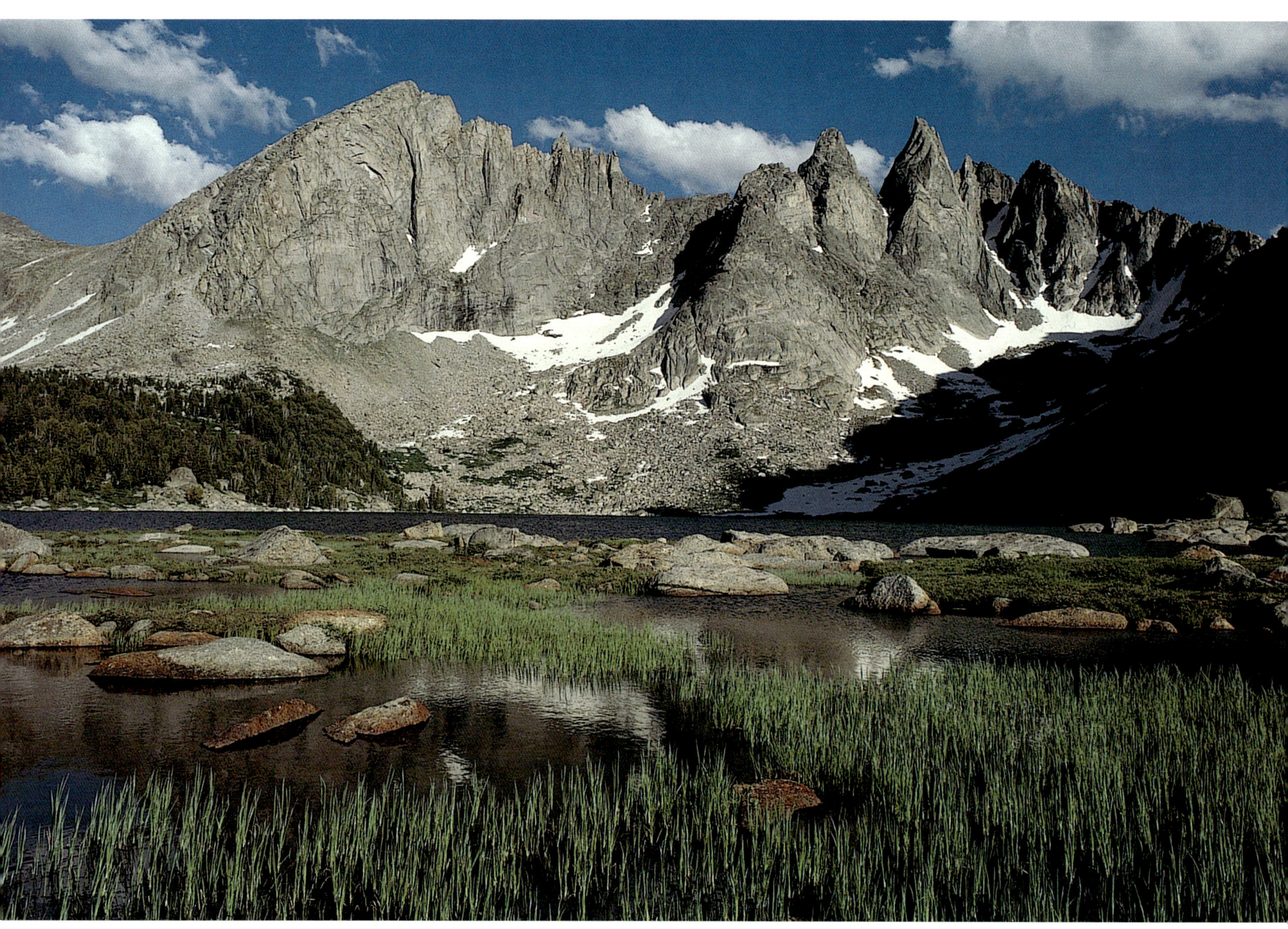

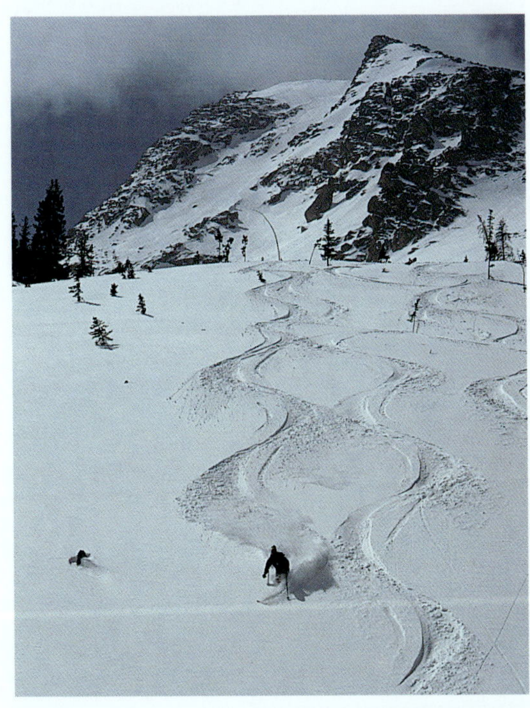

Left: Skiing the powdery slopes below Schiestler Peak.
BEN FRANKLIN

Below: Small, isolated mountain lakes are the favored habitat of the Barrow's goldeneye.
JOHN C. ERIKSSON

Facing page: Bollinger Peak, Overhanging Tower, and Shark's Nose rise from the shore of Shadow Lake, Bridger Wilderness.
DAVID M. MORRIS

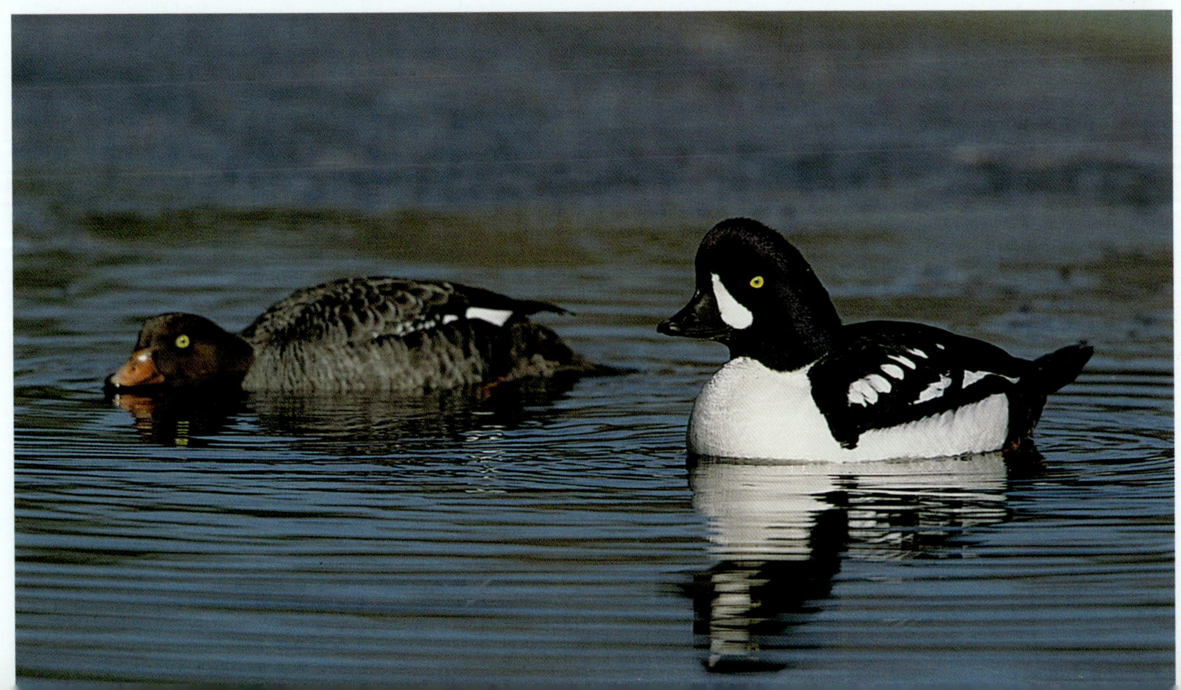

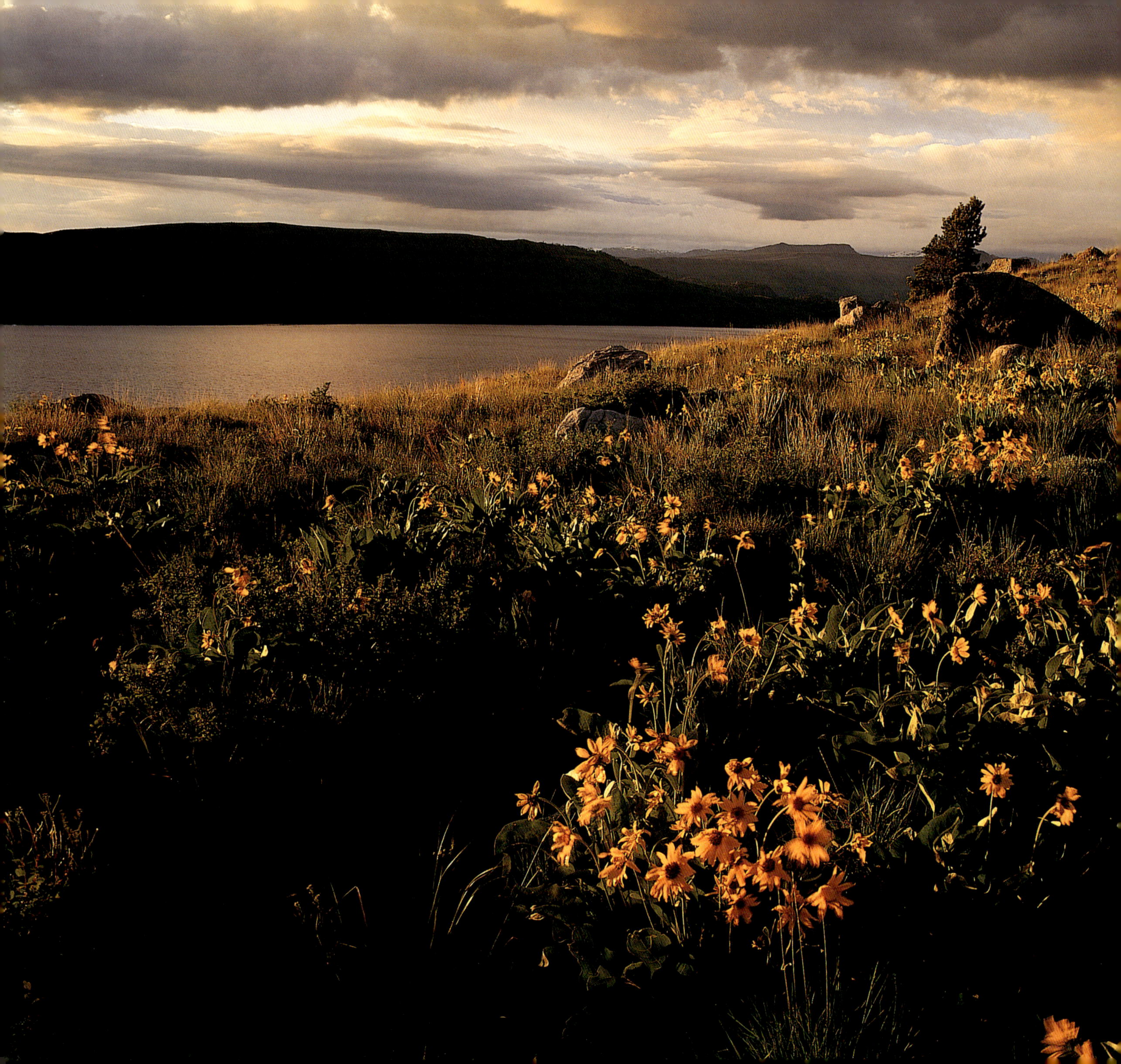

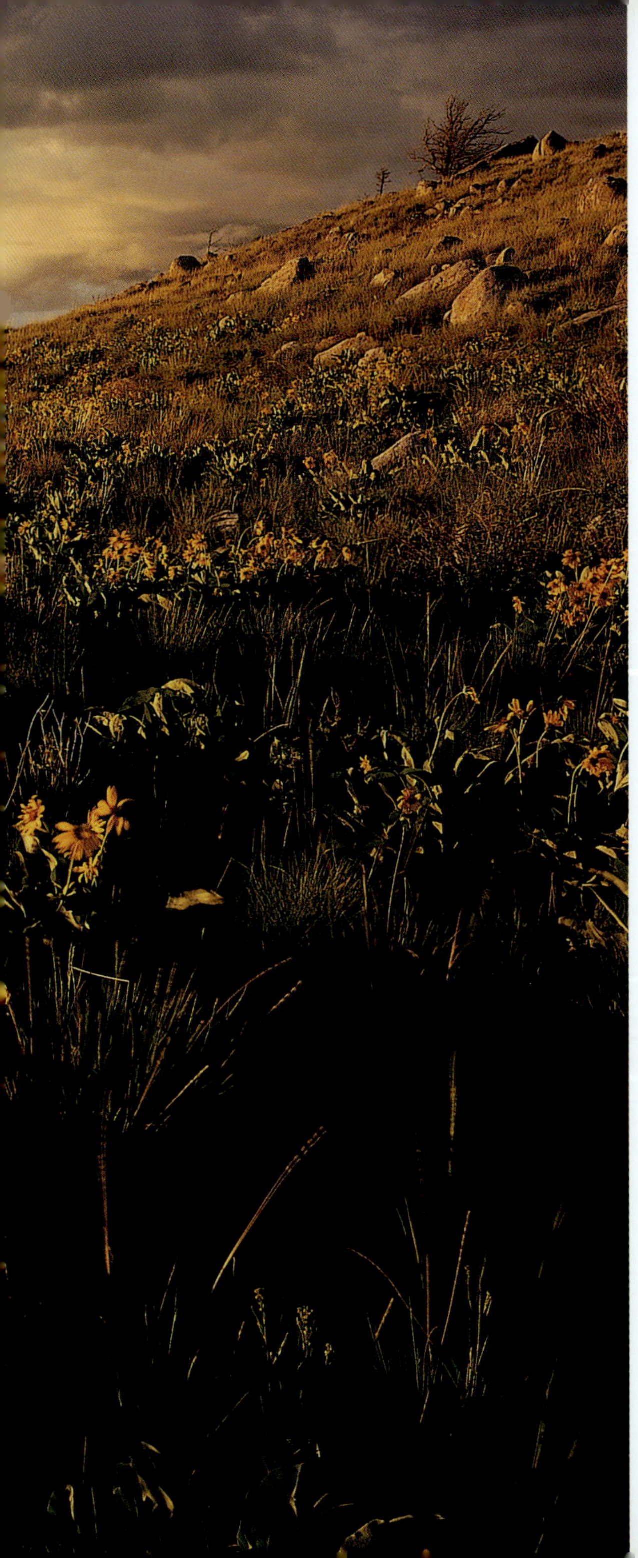

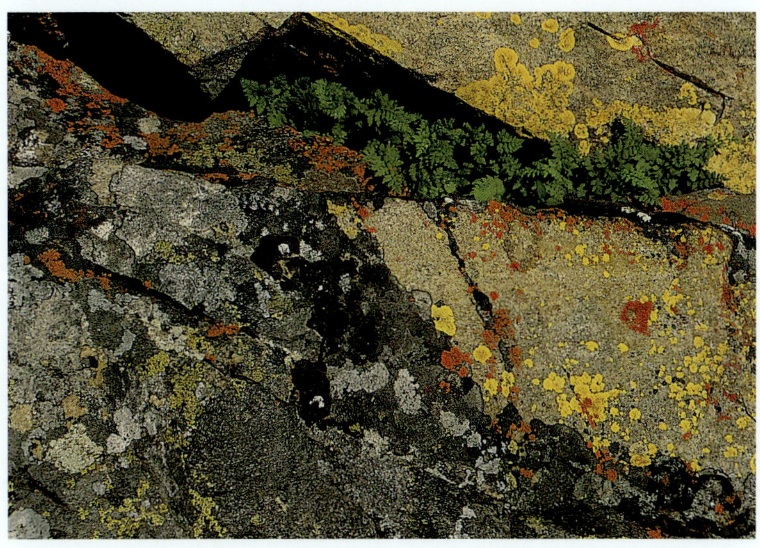

Above: Ferns spread through the crack of a lichen-covered rock.
FRED PFLUGHOFT

Left: The famously cold waters of Fremont Lake, a paradise for anglers, are home to several species of trout and char.
FRED PFLUGHOFT

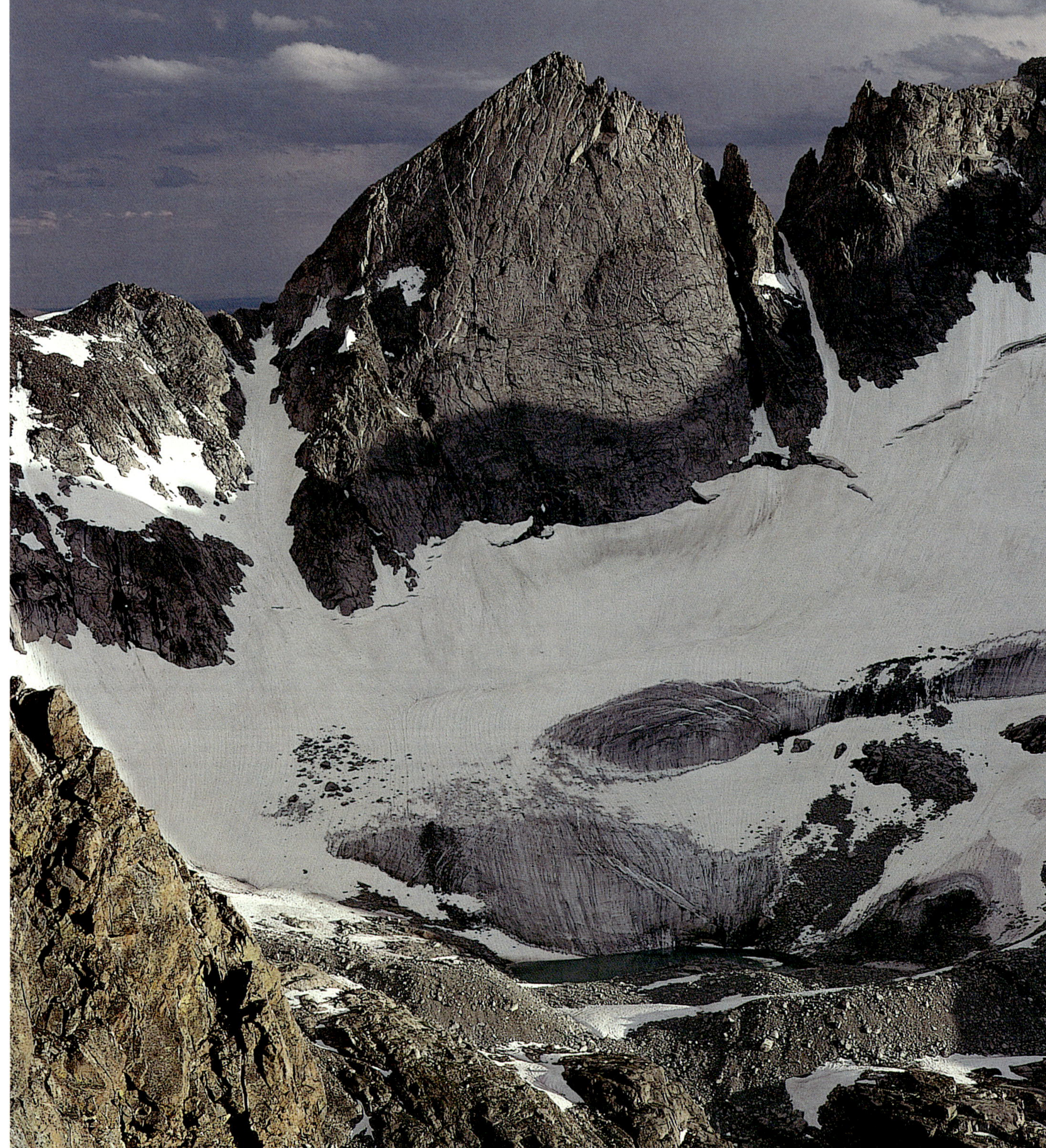

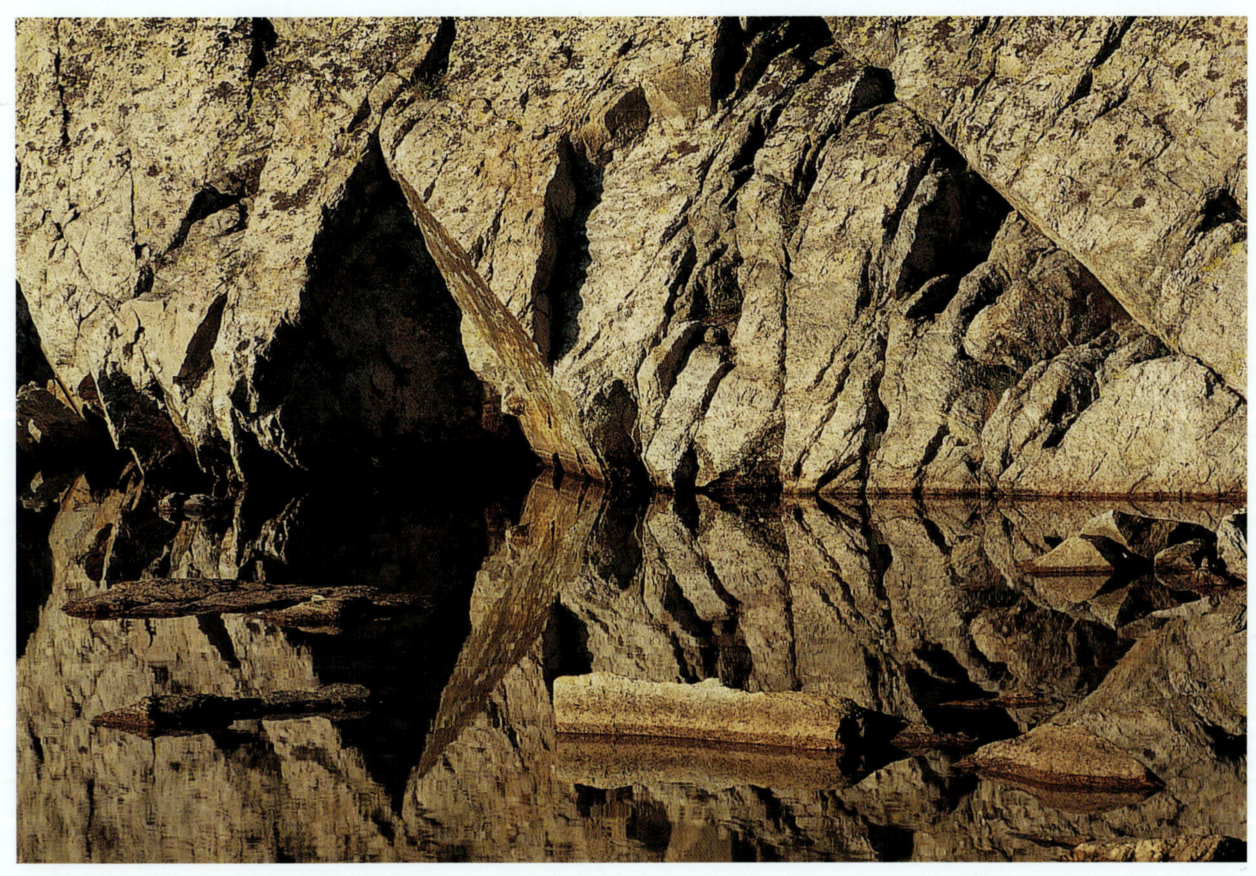

Above: Tarn reflections, Elbow Lake.
FRED PFLUGHOFT

Facing page: Mount Arrowhead rises to an elevation of 12,972 feet. At its foot lies Stroud Glacier, considered by many to be the starting point of the Green River.
FRED PFLUGHOFT

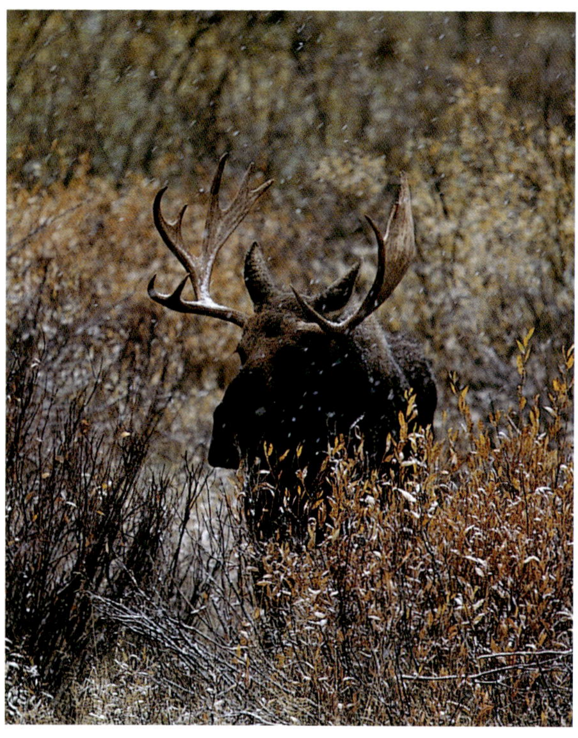

Above: Bull moose in light autumn snowfall.
JOHN L. HINDERMAN

Right: Titcomb Lake, Bridger Wilderness.
FRED PFLUGHOFT

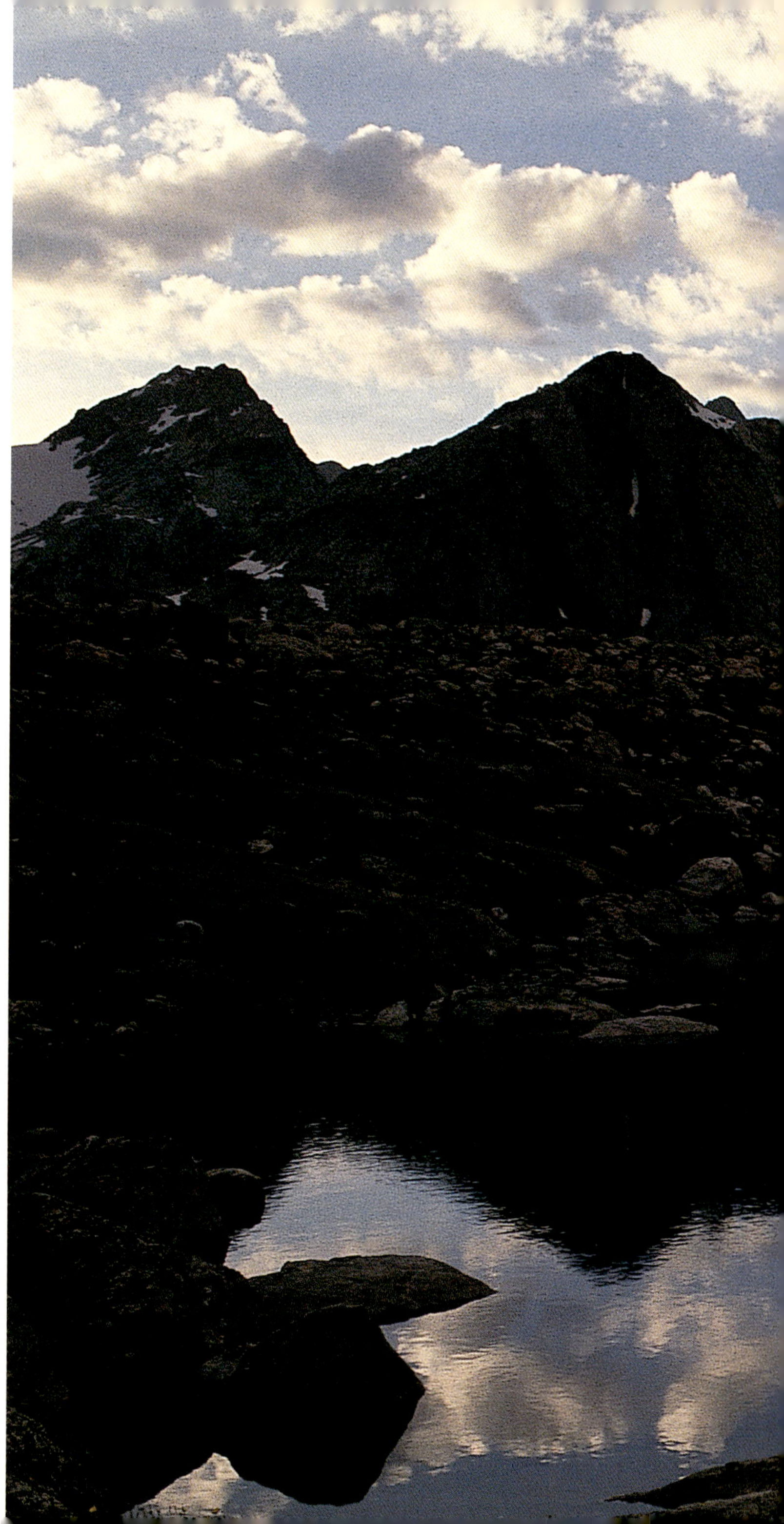

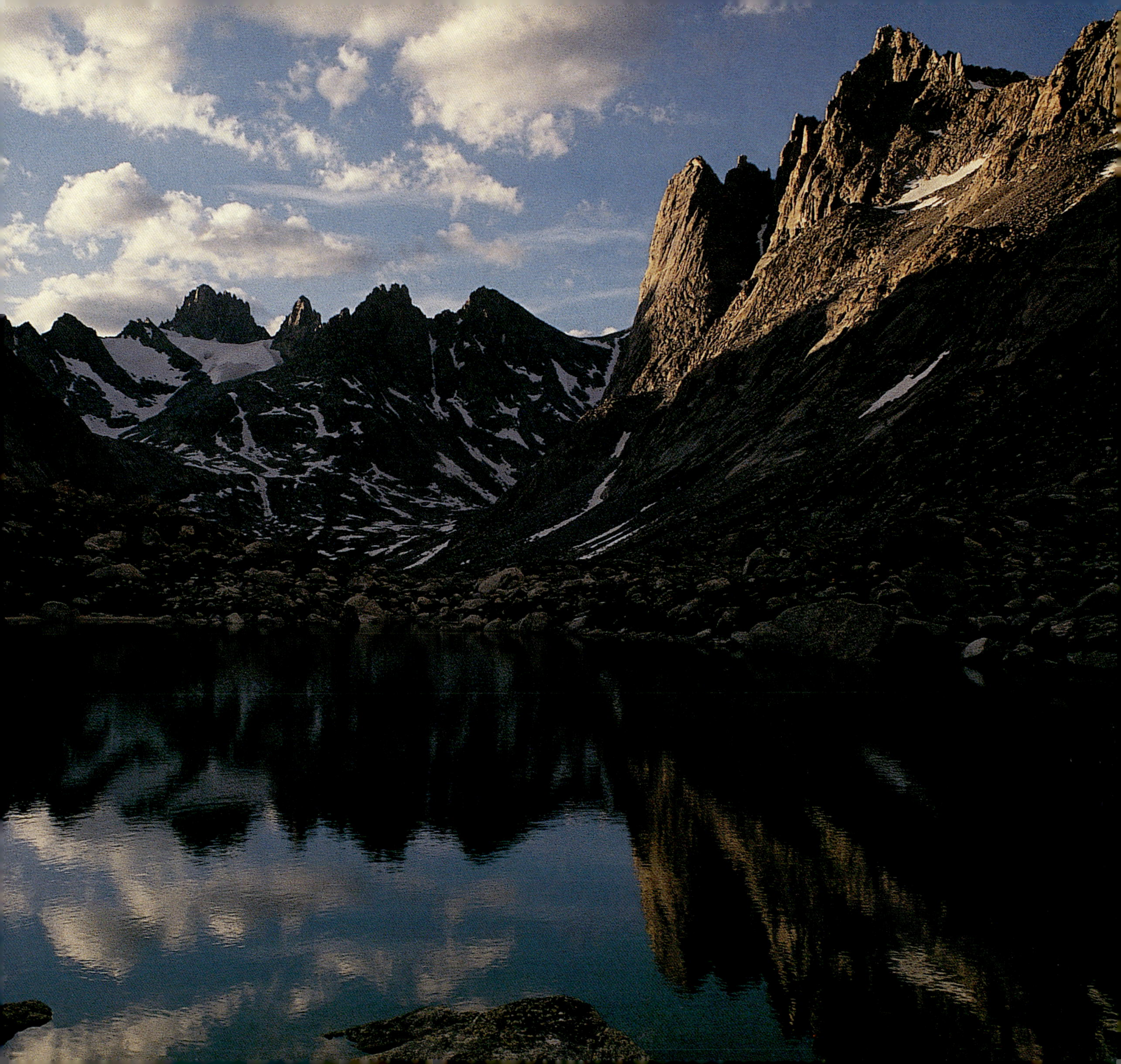

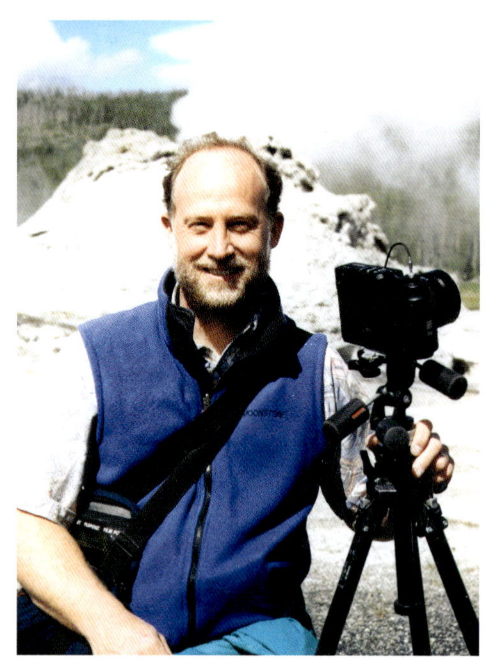

FRED PFLUGHOFT began his professional photography career in 1988 while living in Bend, Oregon. His full-color photography appears regularly in both regional and national magazines ranging from *Montana Magazine* to *Cowboys and Indians* and on calendars and postcards throughout the western United States. He currently has over twenty books in publication, half of them being published by Farcountry Press, including *Grand Teton Wild and Beautiful*, *Wyoming Wild and Beautiful II*, *Yellowstone Wild and Beautiful*, *Washington Impressions*, and *Wyoming's Historic Forts*. You can find out more about his past and current work by visiting fredpflughoftstockphoto.com.

Fred wishes to thank the following photographers for their contributions to *Wind River Range Impressions*:

ELIZABETH BOEHM is a transplant to the Pinedale area who has a deep appreciation for the place she has chosen as home. Her eye for capturing the drama of the intimate landscape is finely honed and rivals that of many of the better-known "intimate landscape" photographers in the United States. You can see more of her exceptional images at wildcolorphotography.com.

DELSA SMITH ALLEN is a native of the Pinedale area whose images bring her own unique perspective to this book. She currently owns and operates her own fine photography and art gallery, Reflections of the Winds, where you can see more of her work. Visit her gallery online at reflectionsofthewinds.com.

BEN FRANKLIN is a native of New Jersey who moved west to Wyoming at the age of seventeen. He owns his own business, Coyote Enterprises, and spends his free time hiking, climbing, backcountry skiing, and photographing throughout western Wyoming. His award-winning photography of this area has appeared in *Wyoming Wildlife* and other regional publications.

JOHN C. ERIKSSON, JOHN L. HINDERMAN, and DAVID M. MORRIS are all-contributing photographers to Fred Pflughoft Stock Photo, and their images have appeared in many of Fred's books as well as in regional and national publications. Their combined talent as photographers is unsurpassed, and they are vital assets to the success of Fred Pflughoft Stock Photo. To see more of their fine work and to learn more about them, visit fredpflughoftstockphoto.com.